# LAURENCE JUBER'S
## DADGAD SOLOS

Performances of these songs can be heard on
Laurence Juber's CD's available from Solid Air Records at
www.AcousticMusicResource.com

For more information on Laurence Juber visit: www.LaurenceJuber.com

Cover photo by Michael Lamont

ISBN 978-1-4803-5460-9

7777 W. BLUEMOUND RD. P.O. BOX 13819 MILWAUKEE, WI 53213

Visit Hal Leonard Online at
**www.halleonard.com**

from *Under an Indigo Sky*

# All the Things You Are

**Lyrics by Oscar Hammerstein II**
**Music by Jerome Kern**

Tuning:
(low to high) D-A-D-G-A-D

**Freely**

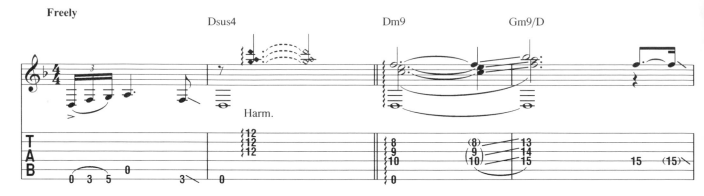

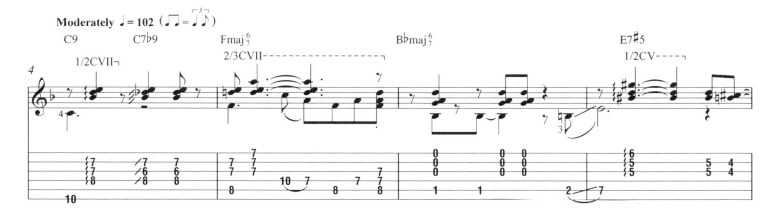

*Artificial Harmonic: The notes are fretted normally and
harmonics are produced by the r.h. tapping the frets
indicated in parentheses.

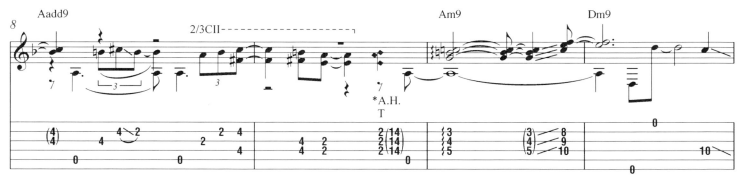

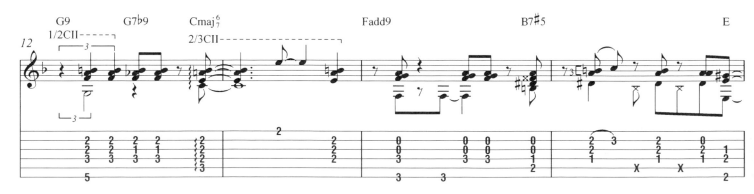

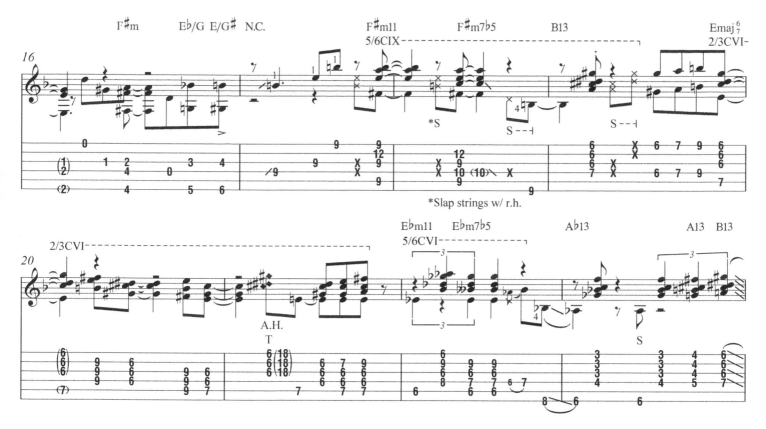

*Slap strings w/ r.h.

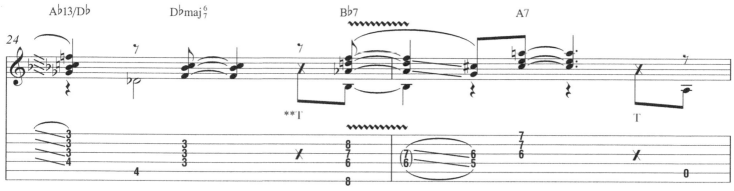

A.H.

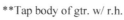

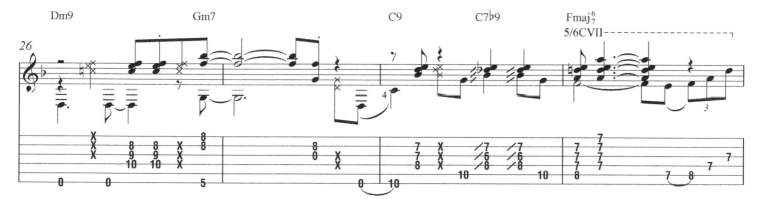

**Tap body of gtr. w/ r.h.

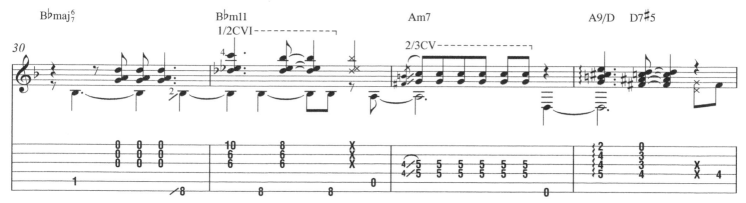

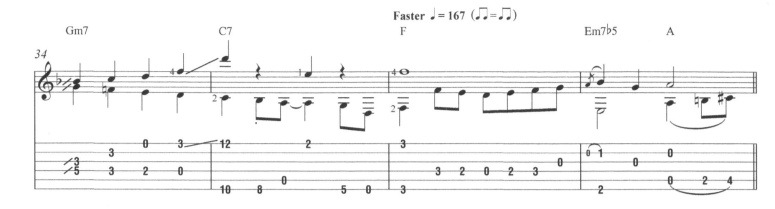

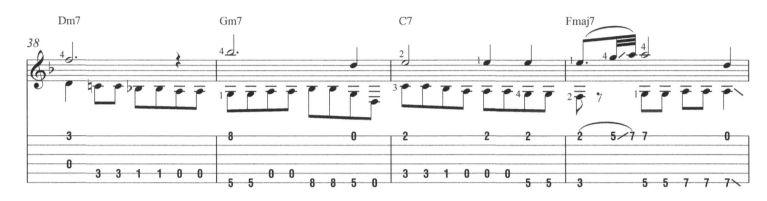

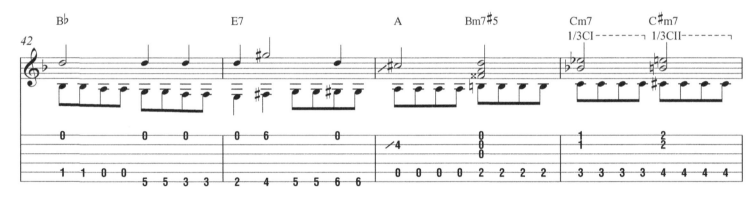

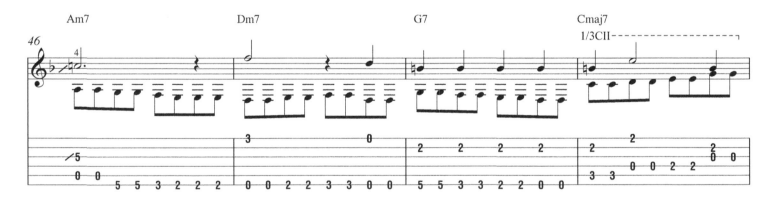

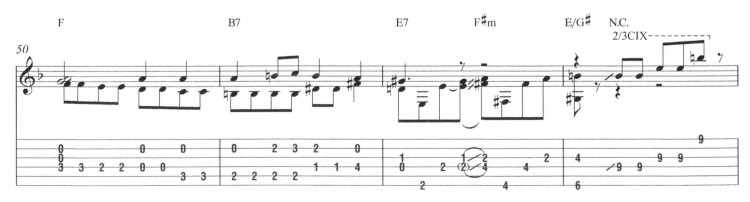

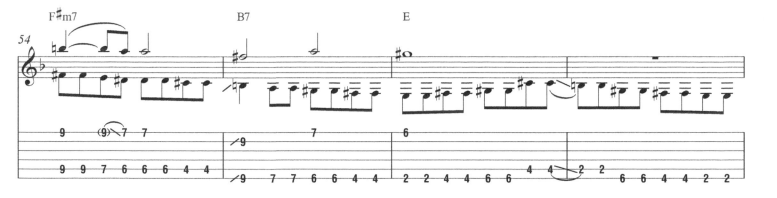

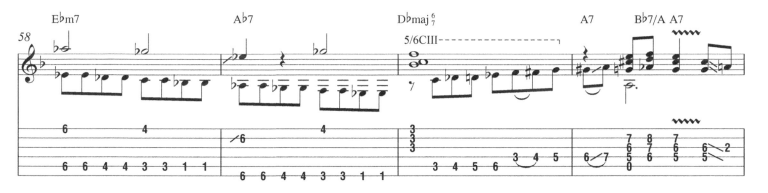

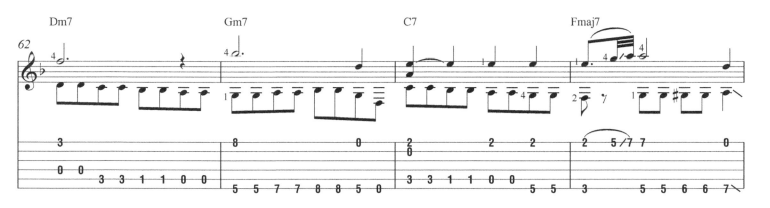

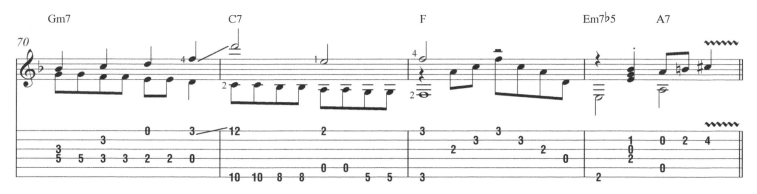

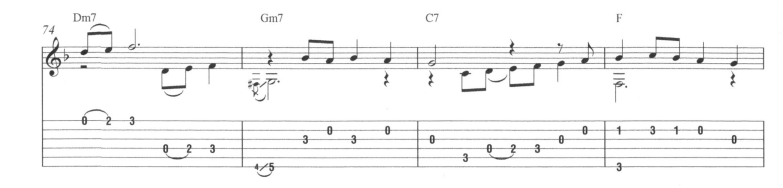

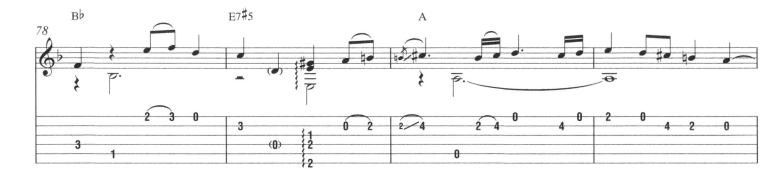

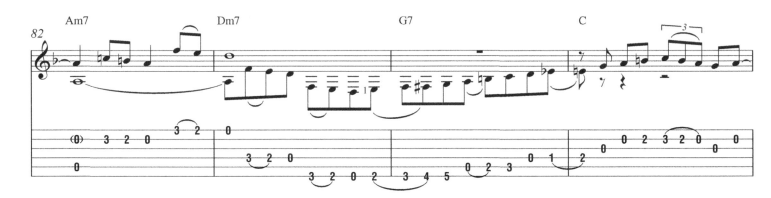

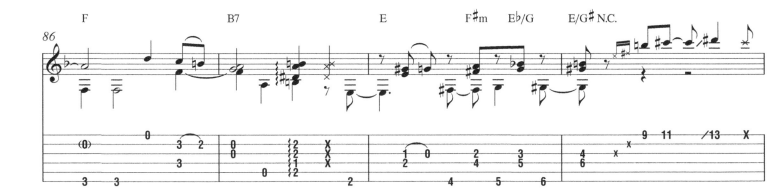

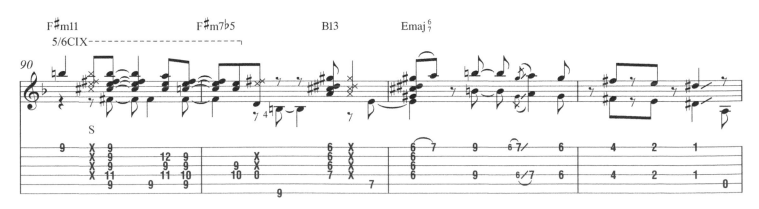

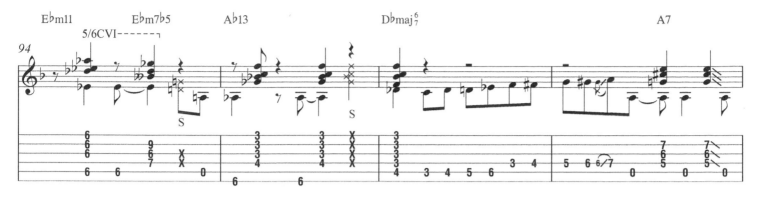

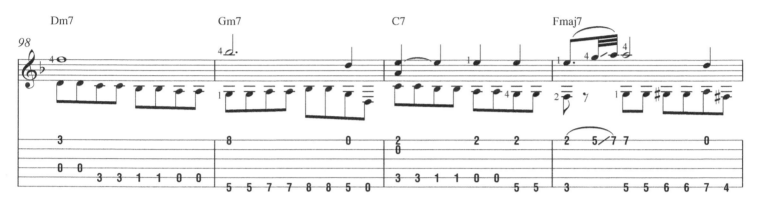

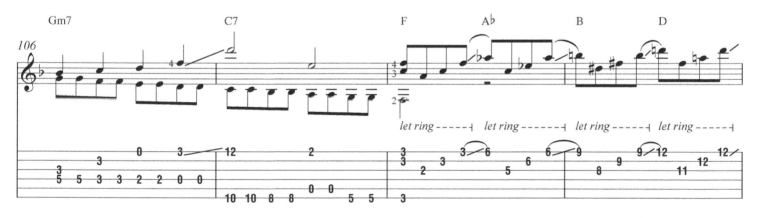

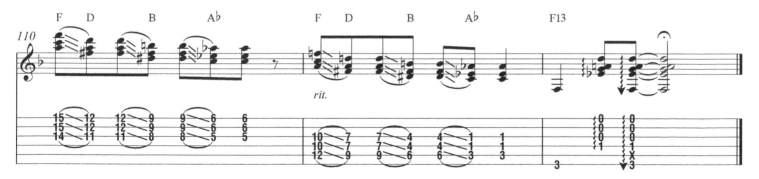

from *Under an Indigo Sky*

# As Time Goes By

**Words and Music by Herman Hupfeld**

Tuning:
(low to high) D-A-D-G-A-D

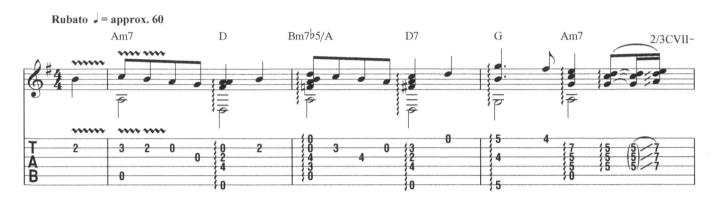

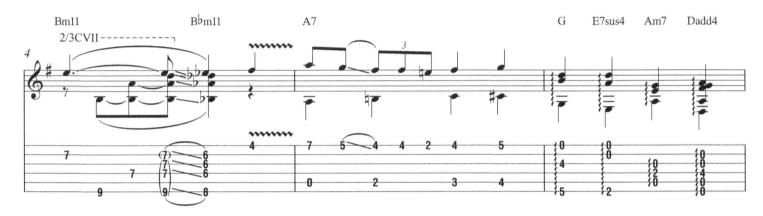

*Artificial Harmonic: The notes are fretted normally and
harmonics are produced by the r.h. tapping the frets
indicated in parentheses.

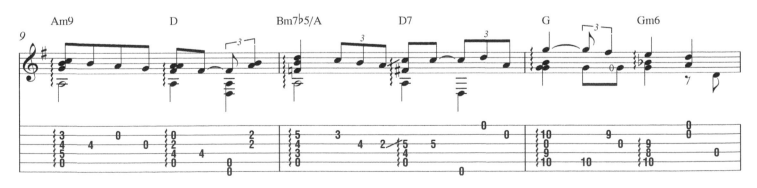

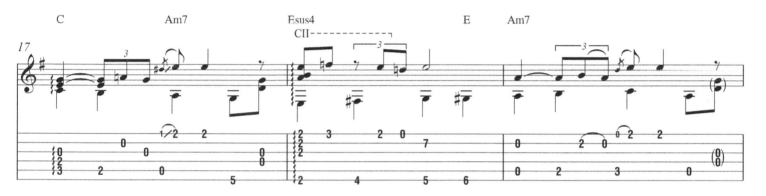

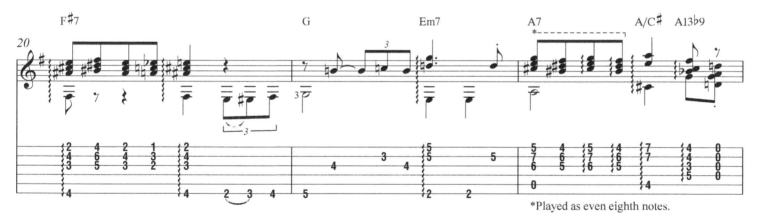

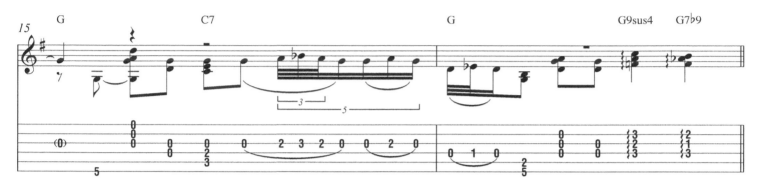

*Played as even eighth notes.

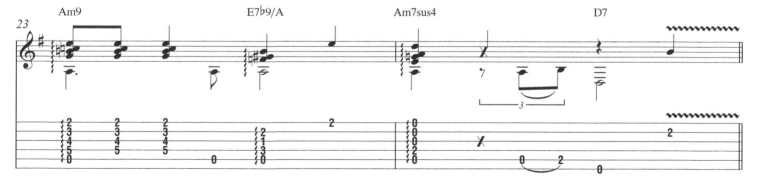

9

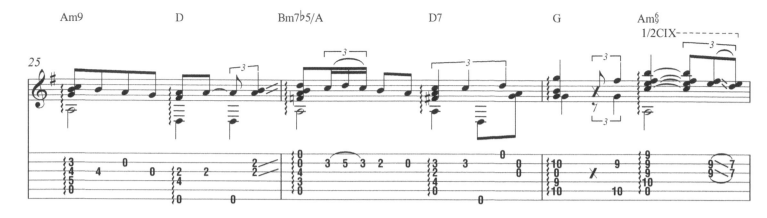

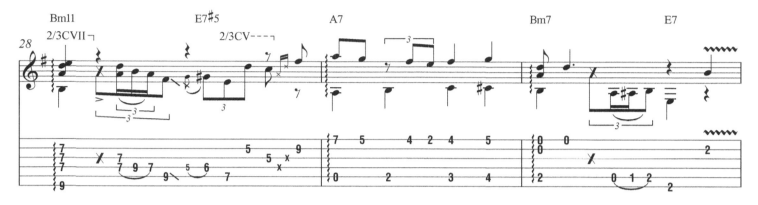

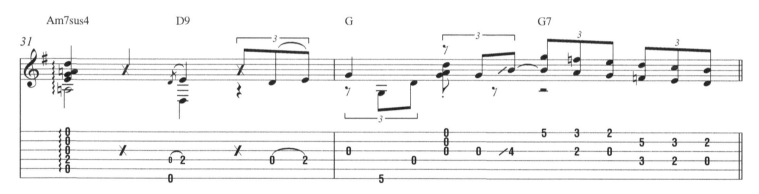

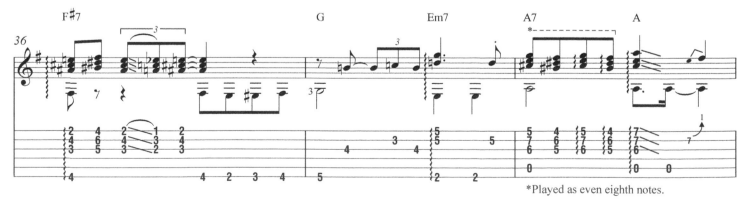

*Played as even eighth notes.

10

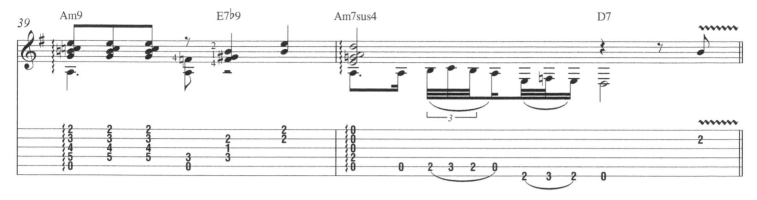

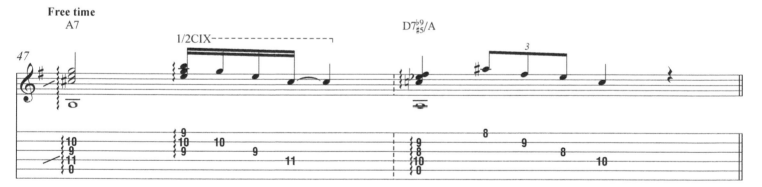

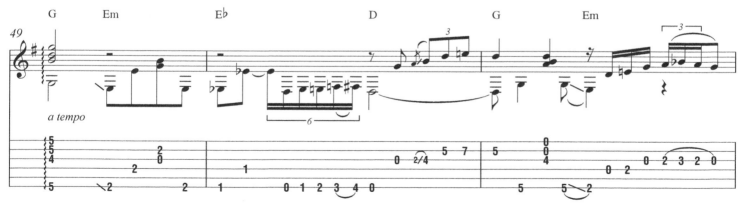

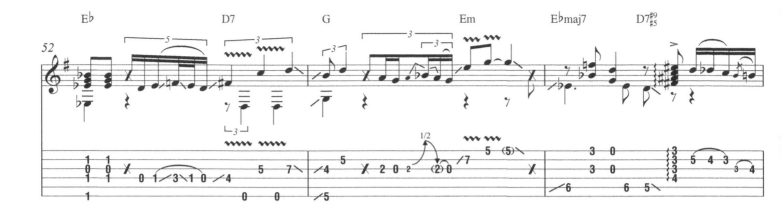

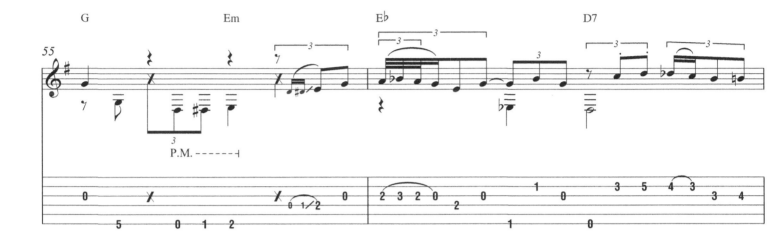

*Played as
  even eighth notes.

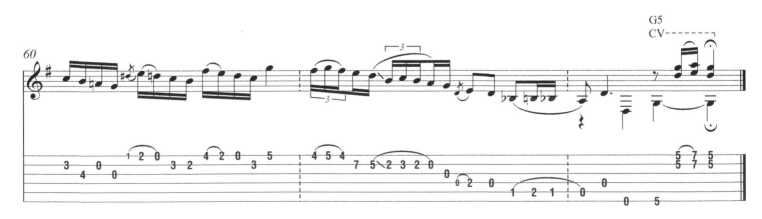

from *Under an Indigo Sky*

# Autumn Leaves

**English lyric by Johnny Mercer**
**French lyric by Jacques Prevert**
**Music by Joseph Kosma**

Tuning:
(low to high) D-A-D-G-A-D

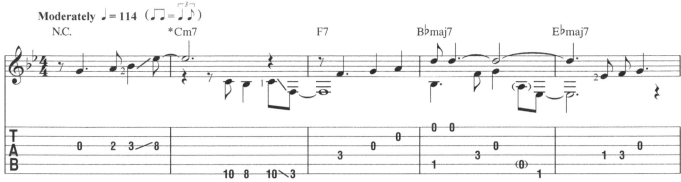

*Chord symbols reflect implied harmony.

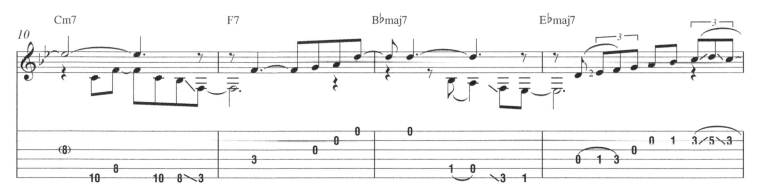

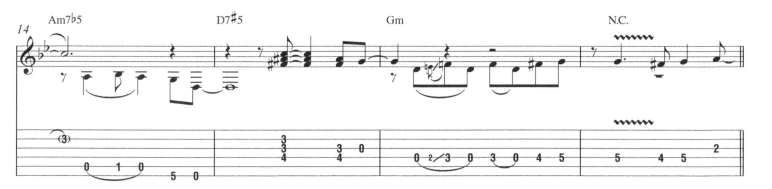

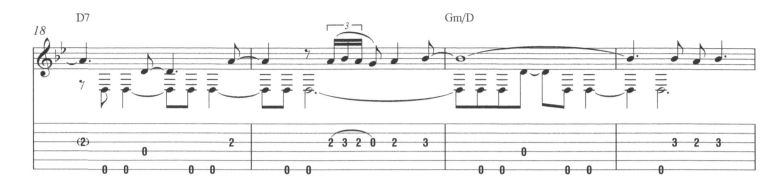

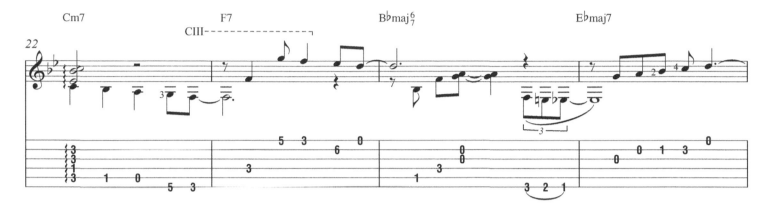

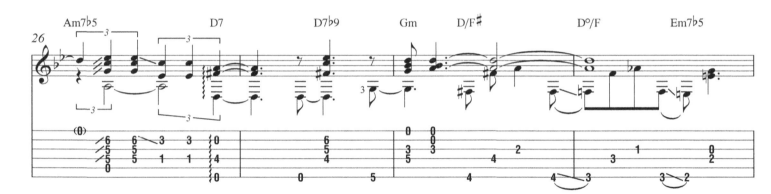

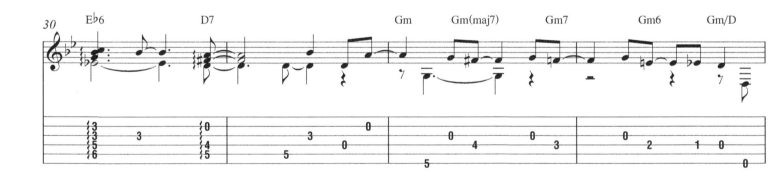

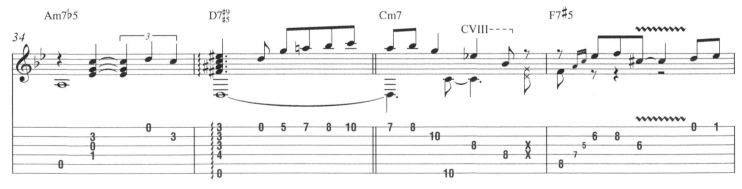

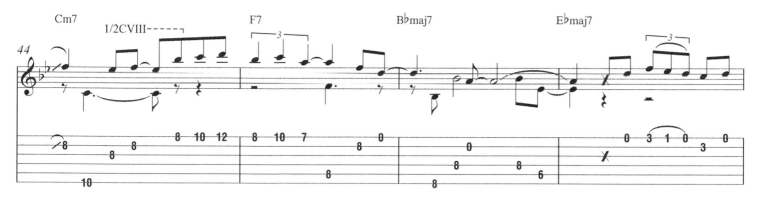

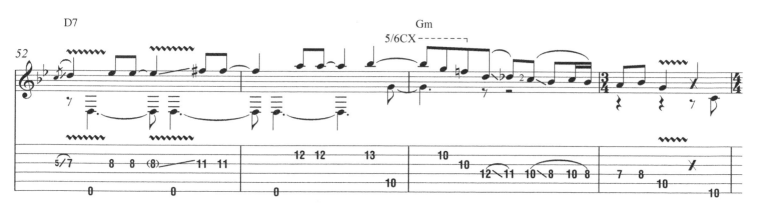

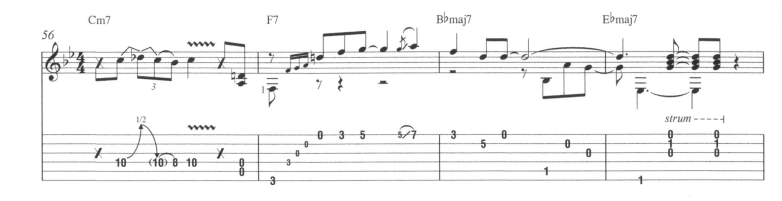

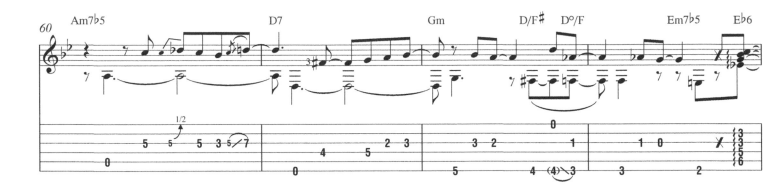

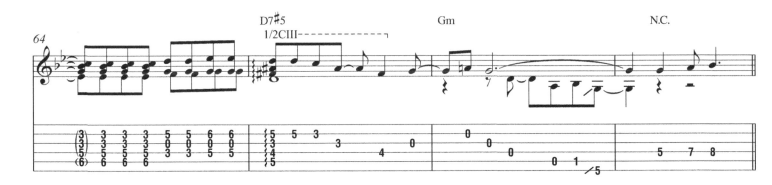

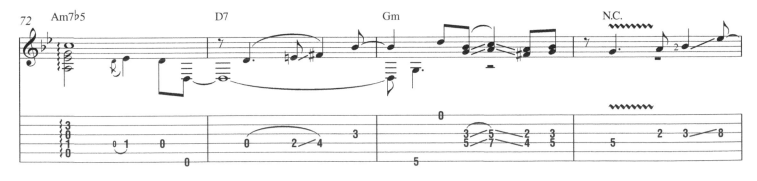

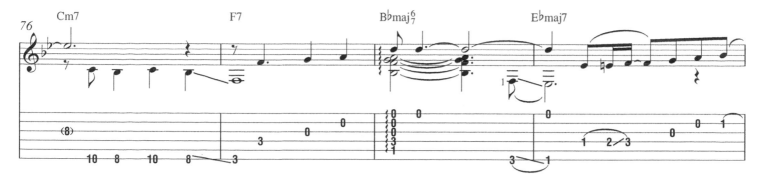

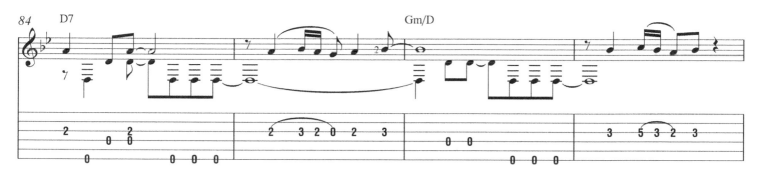

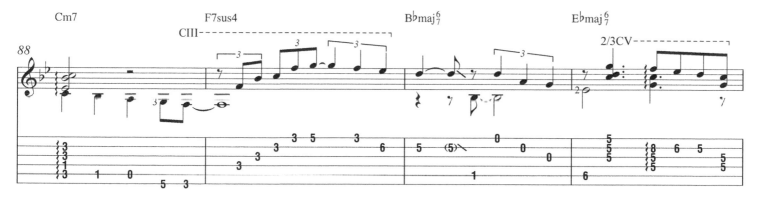

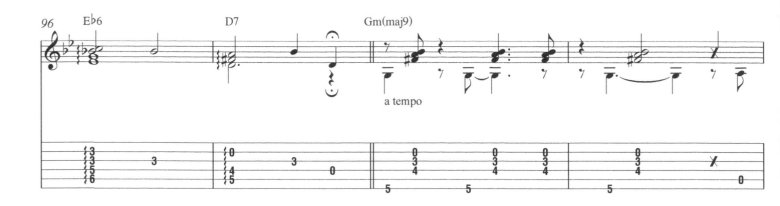

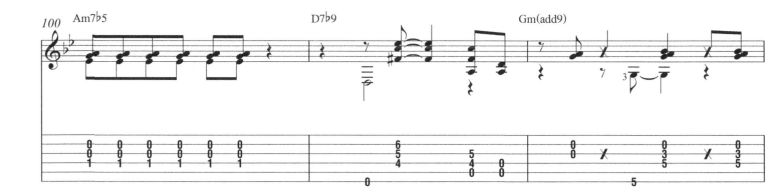

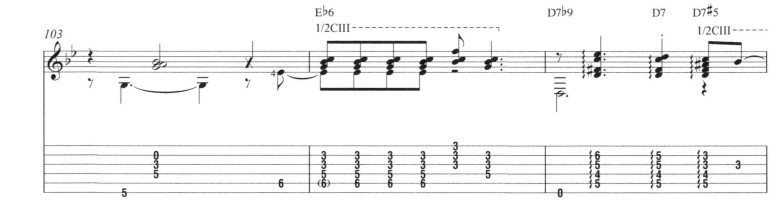

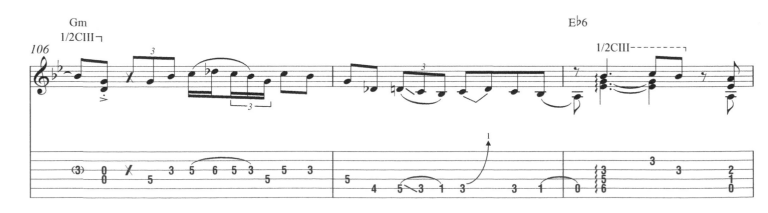

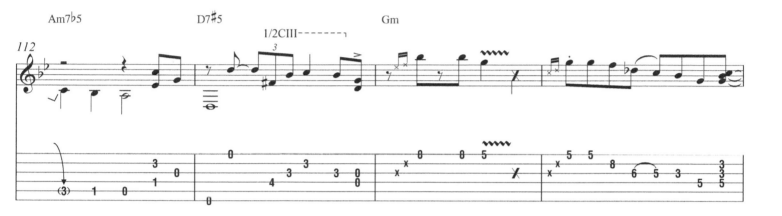

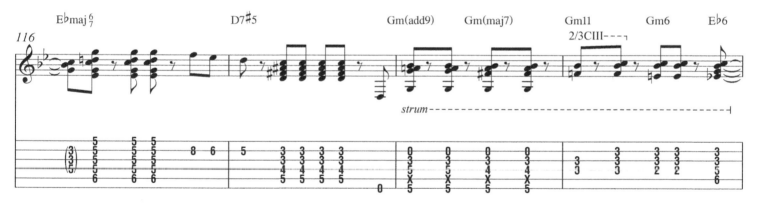

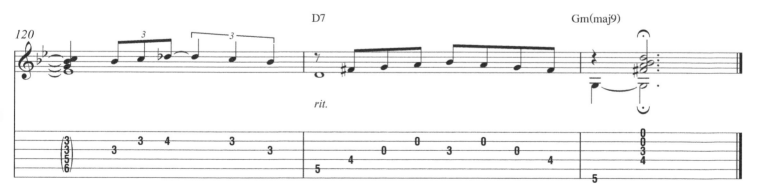

# Come Rain or Come Shine

**Words by Johnny Mercer**
**Music by Harold Arlen**

Tuning:
(low to high) D-A-D-G-A-D

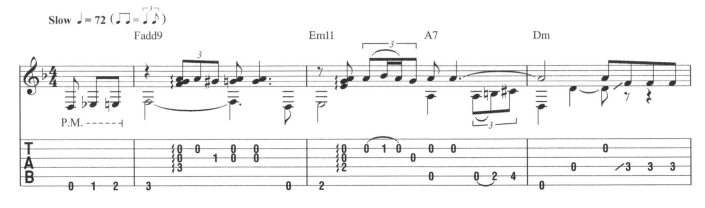

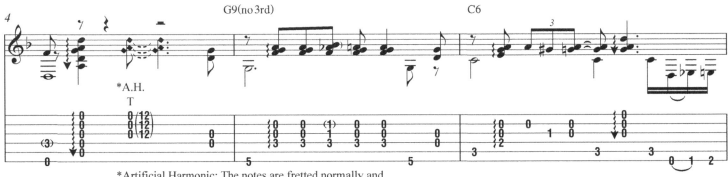

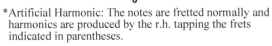

*Artificial Harmonic: The notes are fretted normally and
harmonics are produced by the r.h. tapping the frets
indicated in parentheses.

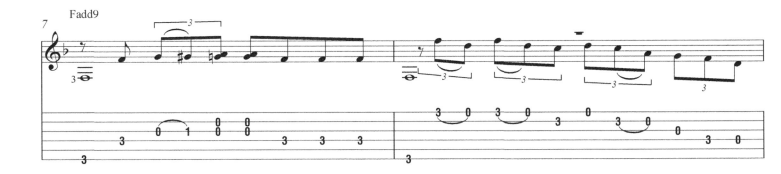

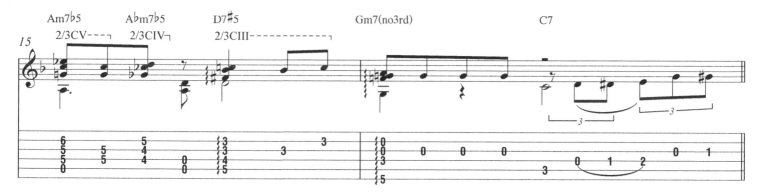

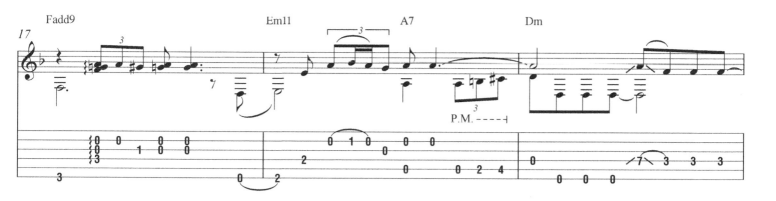

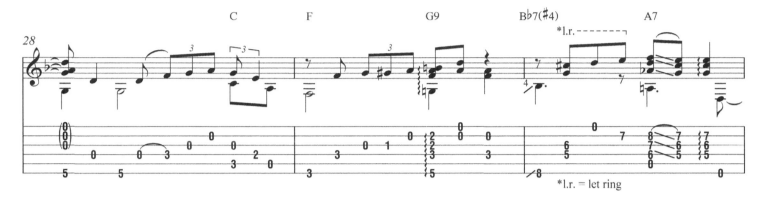

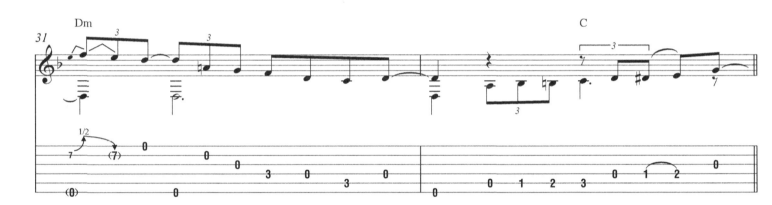

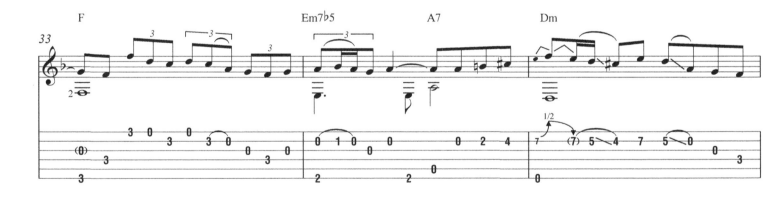

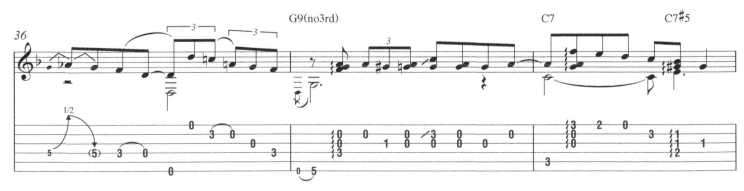

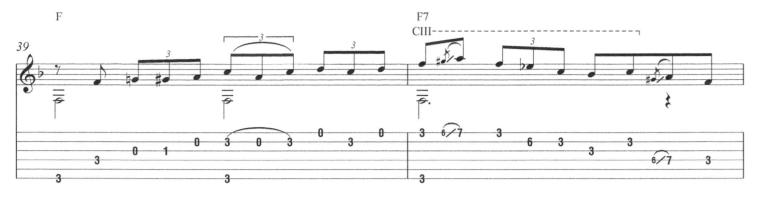

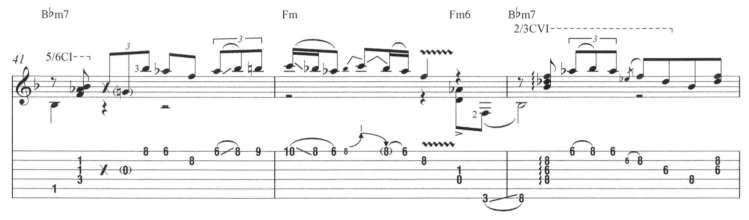

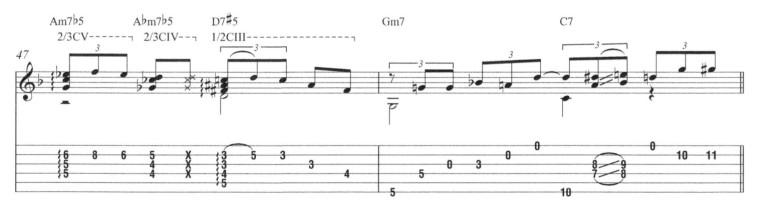

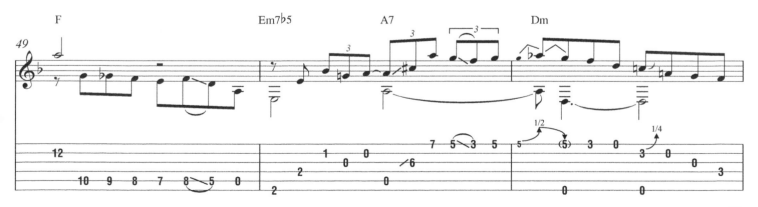

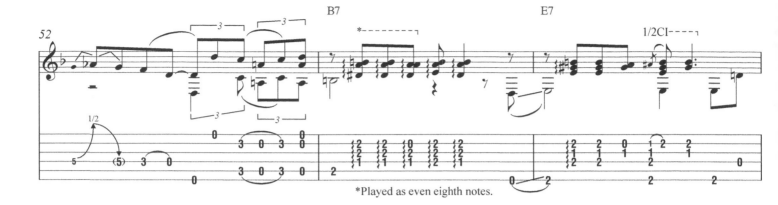

*Played as even eighth notes.

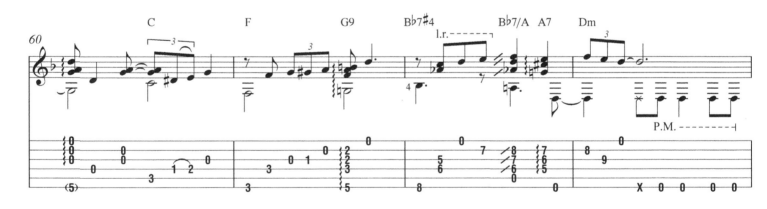

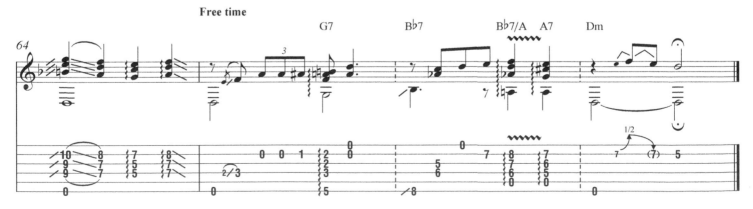

from *Under an Indigo Sky*

# Don't Let Me Be Misunderstood

**Words and Music by Bennie Benjamin, Sol Marcus and Gloria Caldwell**

Tuning:
(low to high) D-A-D-G-A-D

♩ = 100

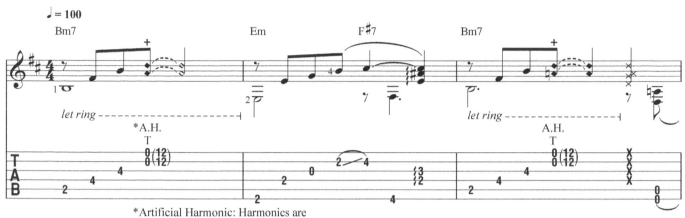

*Artificial Harmonic: Harmonics are
produced by the r.h. tapping at the 12th fret.

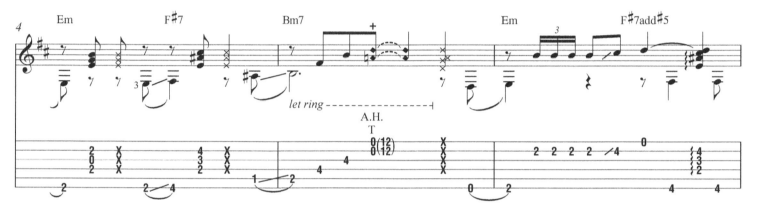

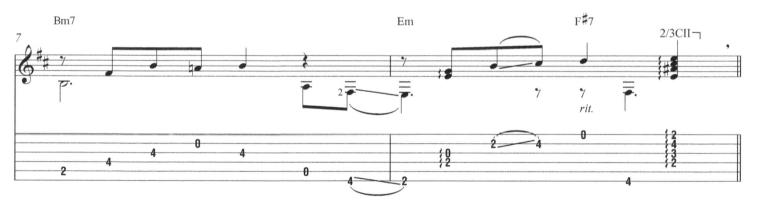

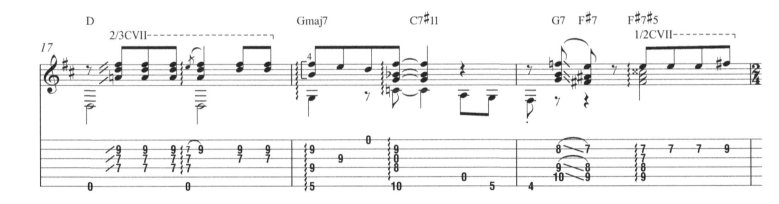

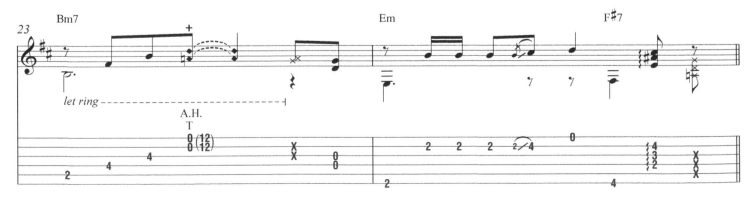

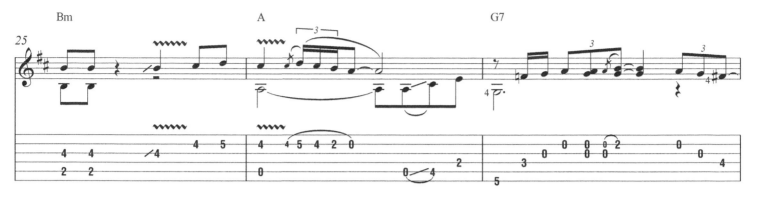

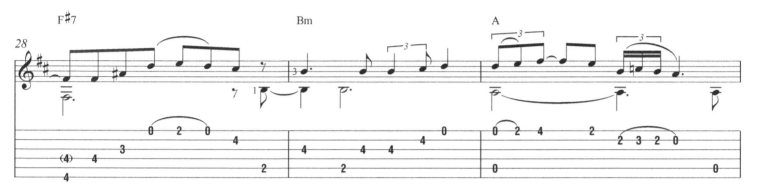

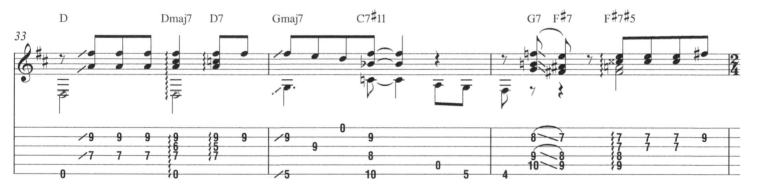

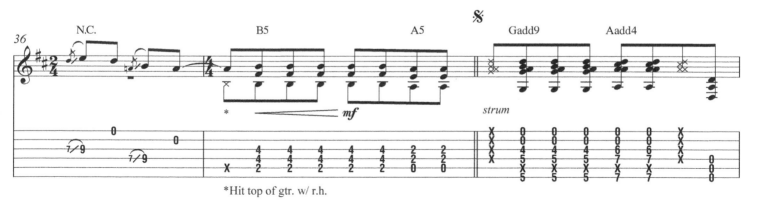

*Hit top of gtr. w/ r.h.

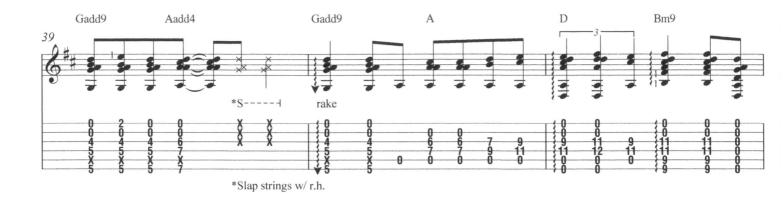

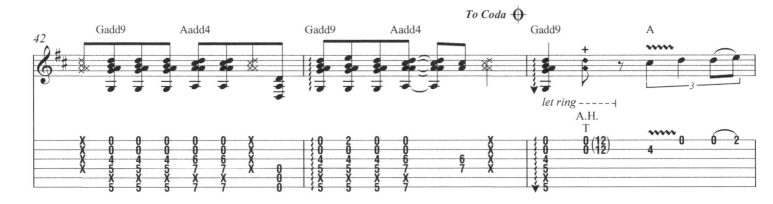

*Slap strings w/ r.h.

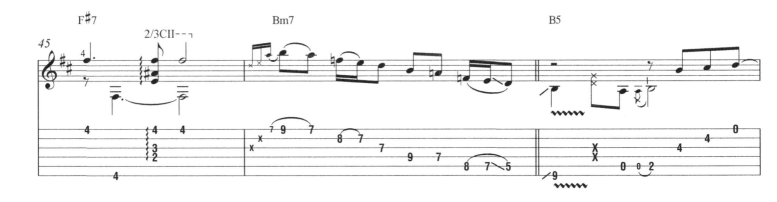

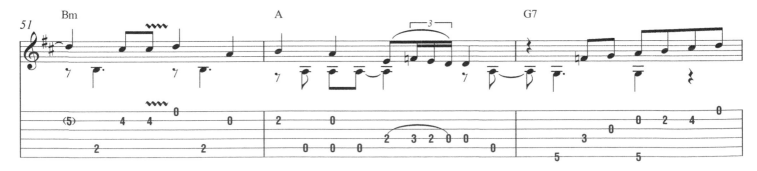

D.S. al Coda

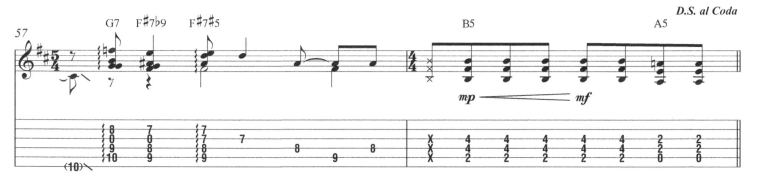

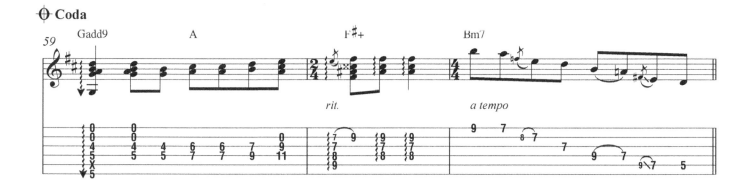

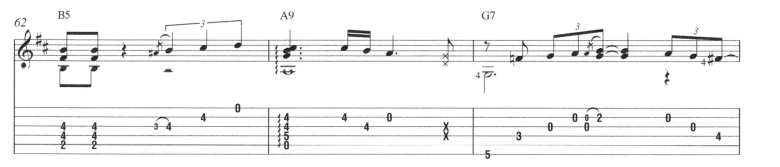

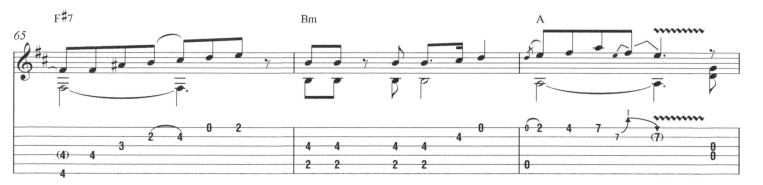

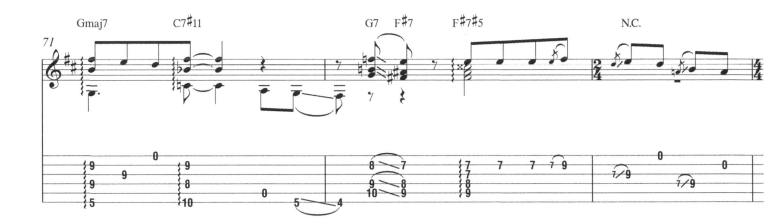

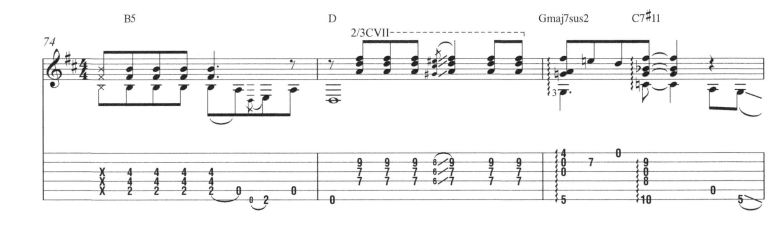

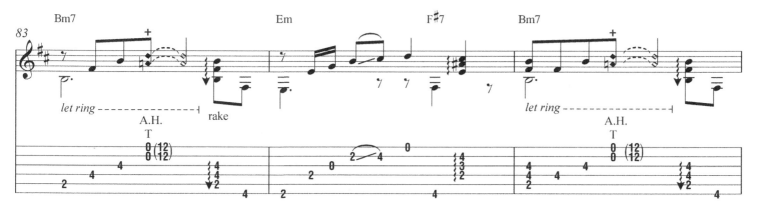

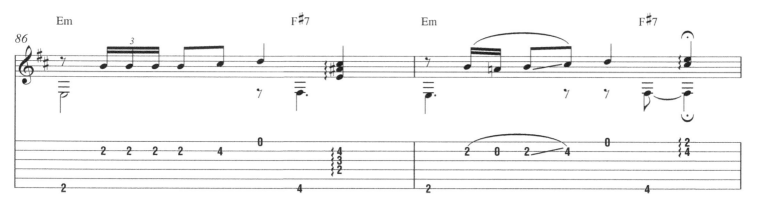

from *Under an Indigo Sky*

# Cry Me a River

**Words and Music by Arthur Hamilton**

Tuning:
(low to high) D-A-D-G-A-D

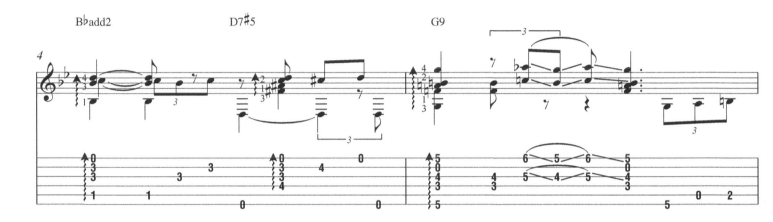

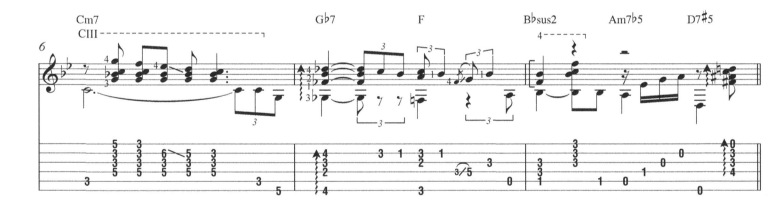

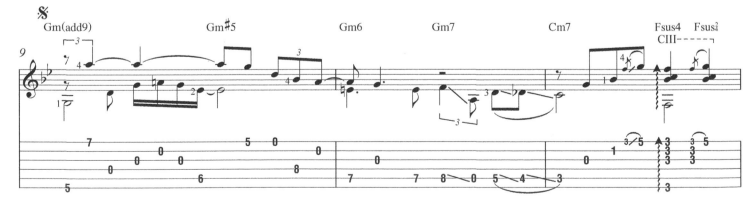

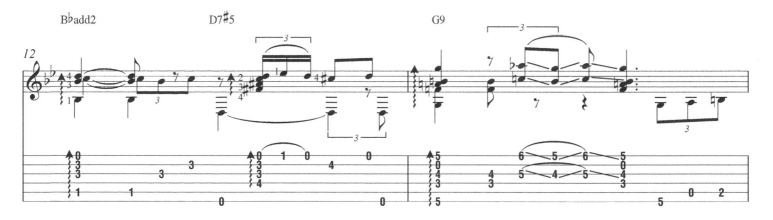

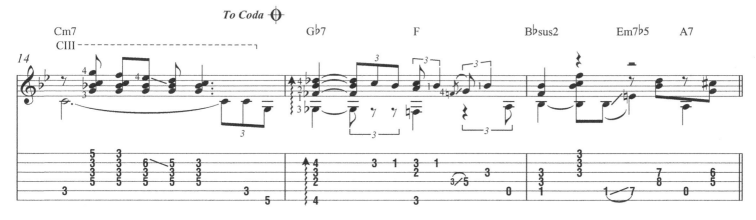

*To Coda* ⊕

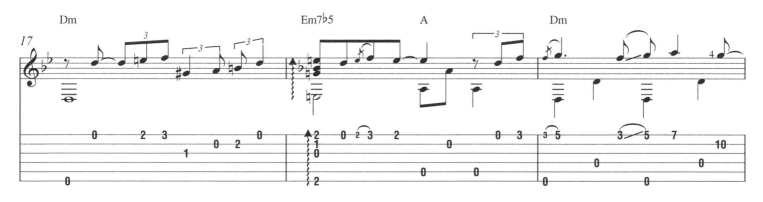

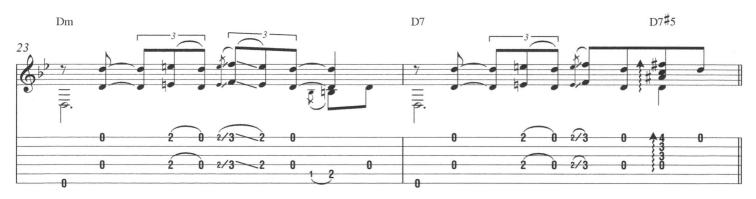

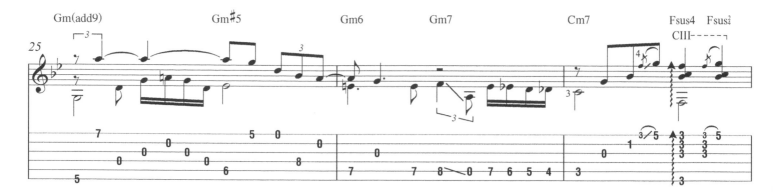

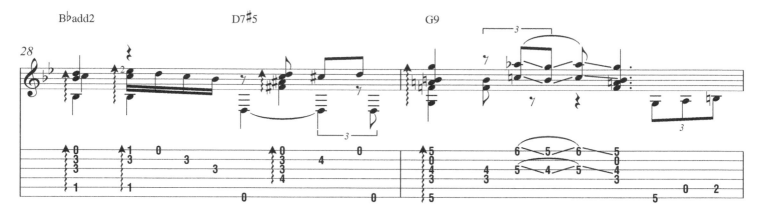

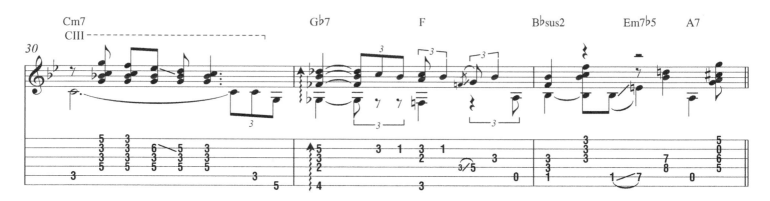

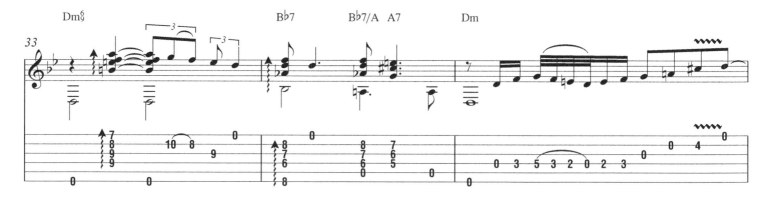

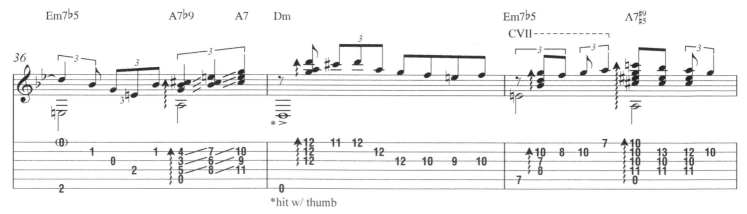

*hit w/ thumb

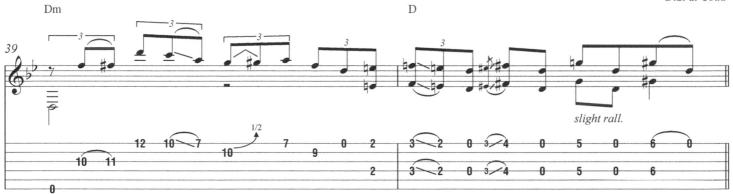

**⊕ Coda**

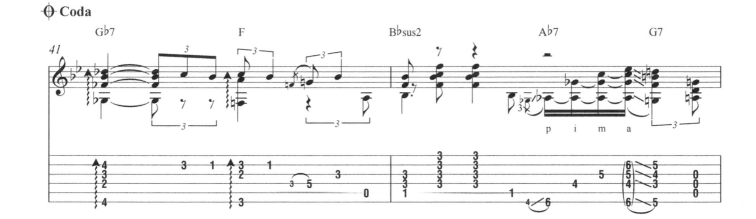

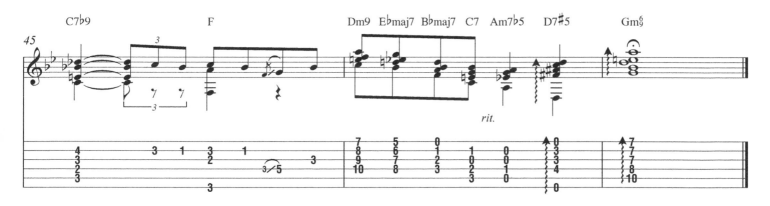

from *Fingerboard Road*

# Georgia on My Mind

**Words by Stuart Gorrell**
**Music by Hoagy Carmichael**

Tuning:
(low to high) D-A-D-G-A-D

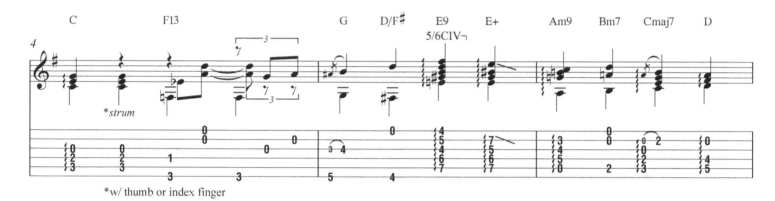

*strum

*w/ thumb or index finger

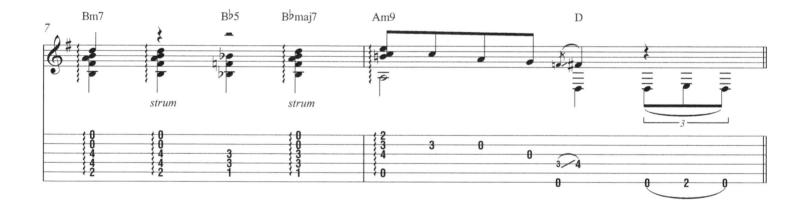

*Artificial Harmonic: Harmonics are
produced by the r.h. tapping at the 12th fret.

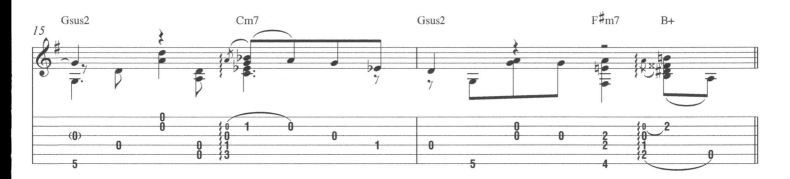

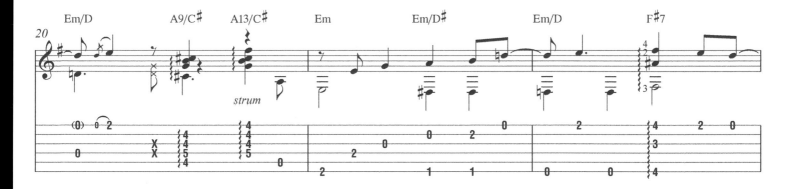

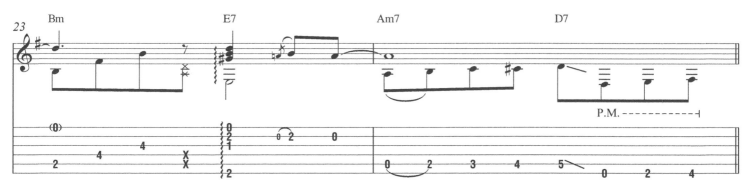

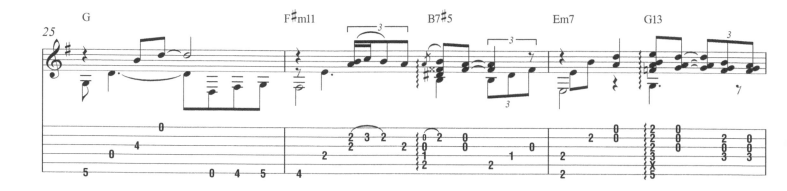

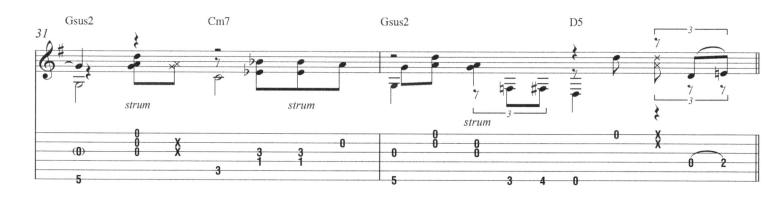

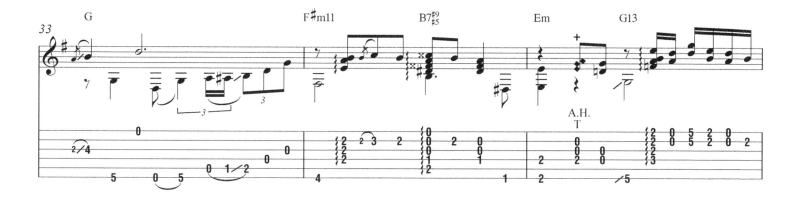

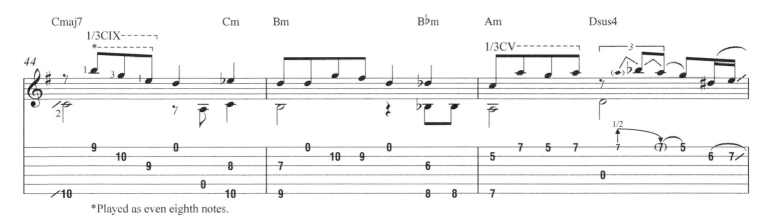

*Played as even eighth notes.

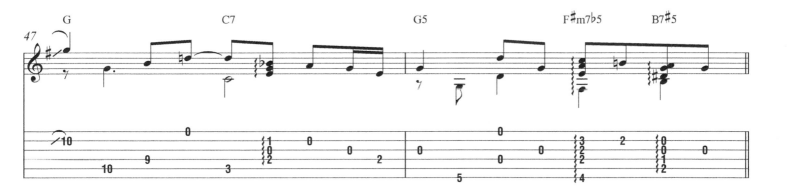

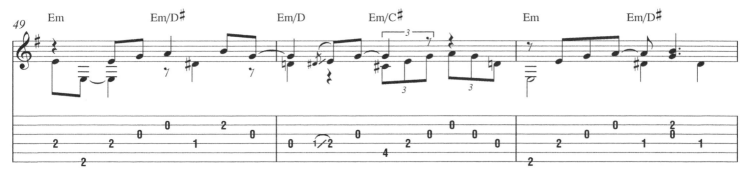

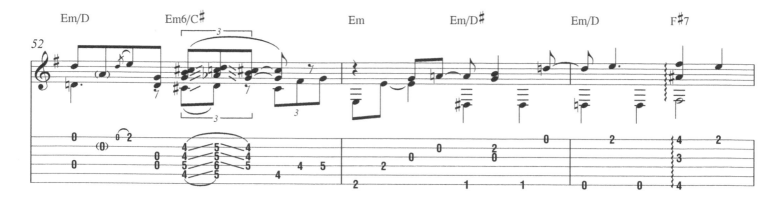

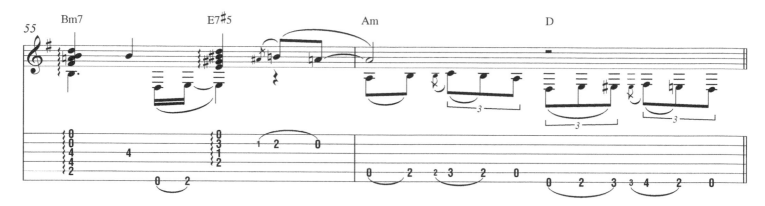

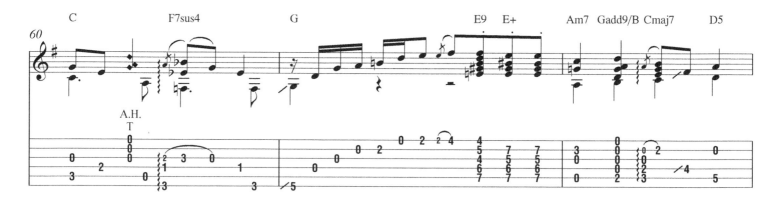

*Played as even eighth notes.

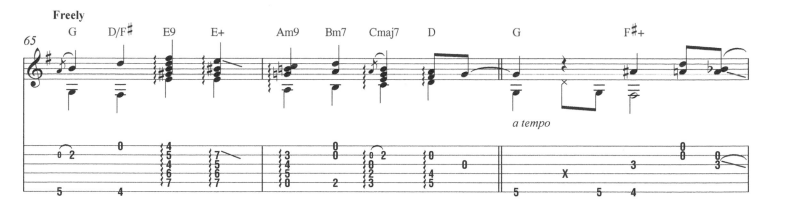

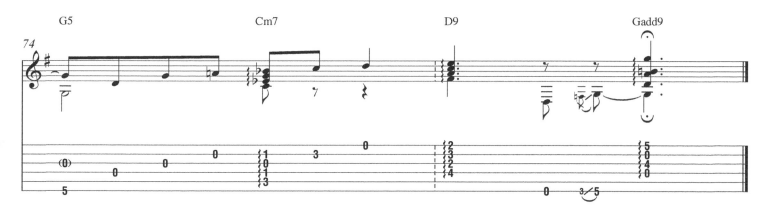

from *I've Got the World on Six Strings*

# Over the Rainbow

from THE WIZARD OF OZ
Music by Harold Arlen
Lyric by E.Y. "Yip" Harburg

Tuning:
(low to high) D-A-D-G-A-D

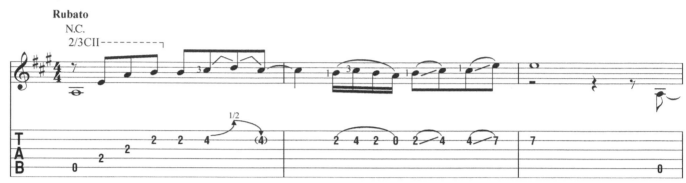

*Harp Harmonic: The note is fretted normally and a harmonic is produced by gently resting the right hand's index finger
12 frets (one octave) above the indicated fret while the right hand's thumb assists by plucking the appropriate string.
This technique also applies to unfretted harmonics played at the 12th fret.

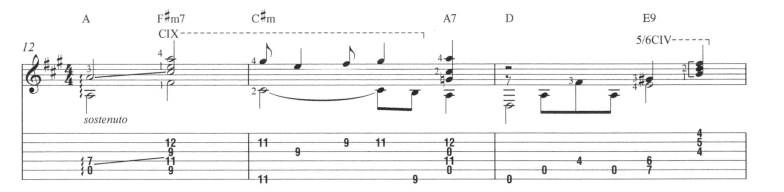

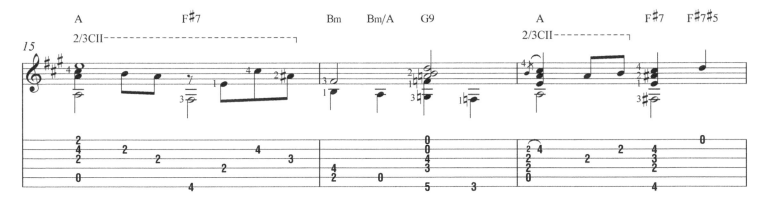

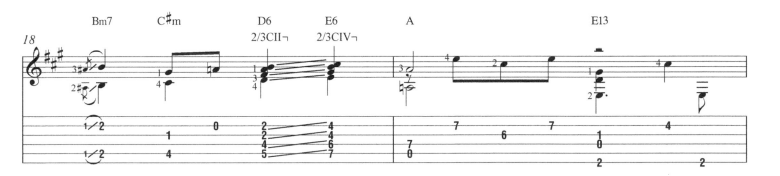

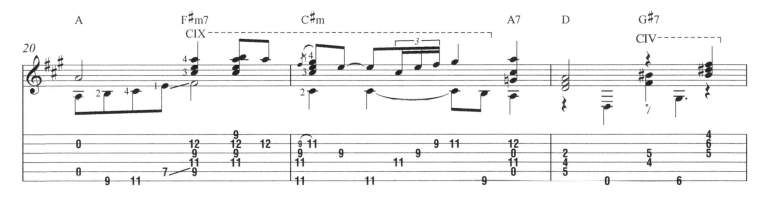

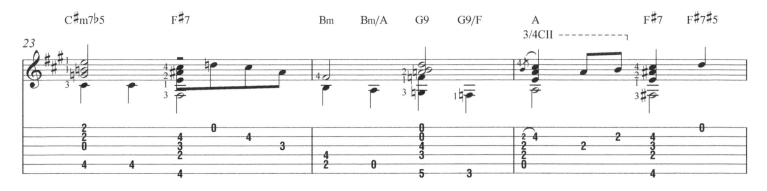

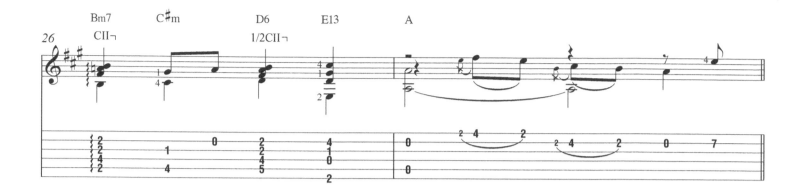

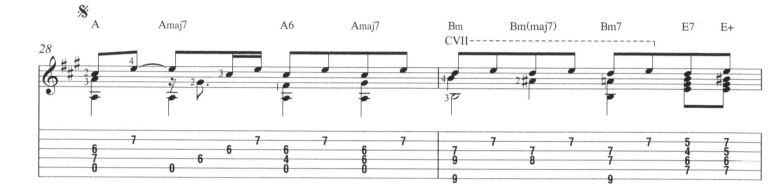

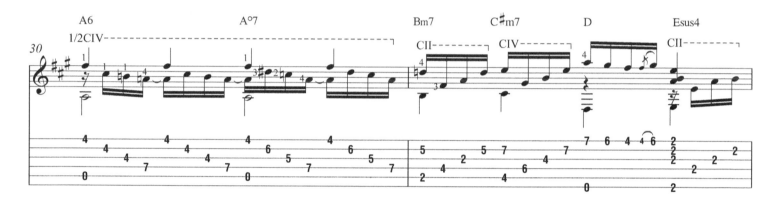

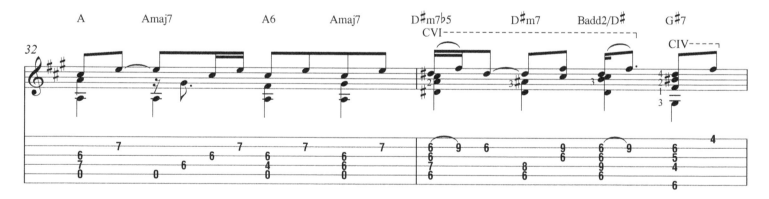

*To Coda* ⊕

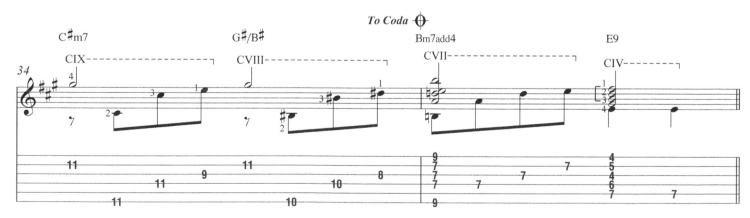

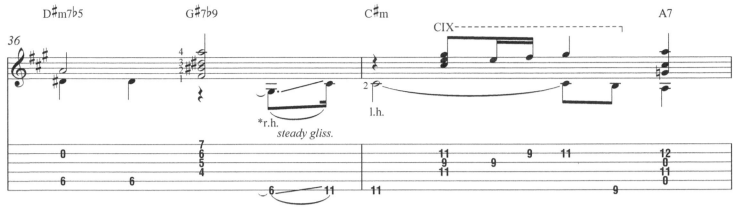

*r.h.
*steady gliss.*

*r.h middle finger hammer & slide

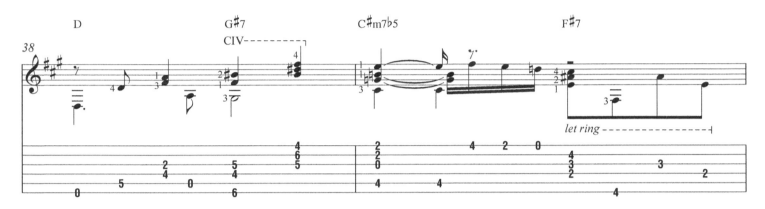

let ring - - - - - - - - - - - - - - -

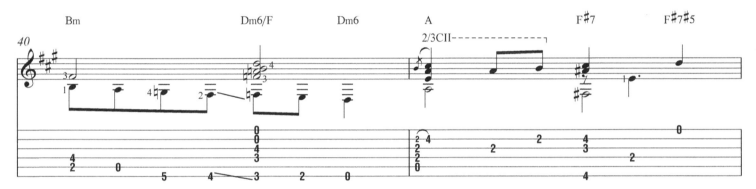

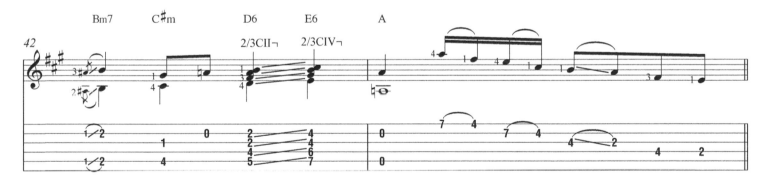

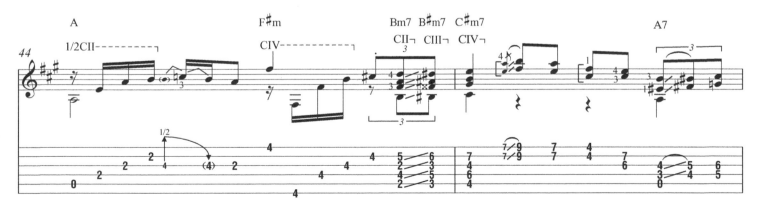

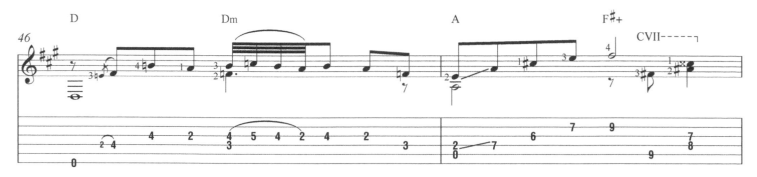

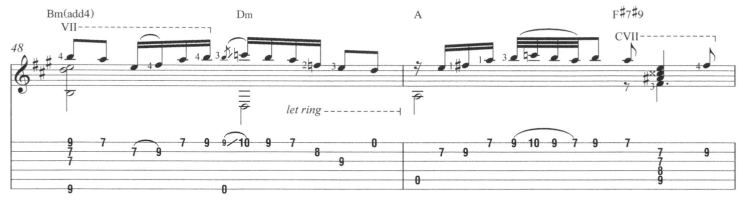

*D.S. al Coda*

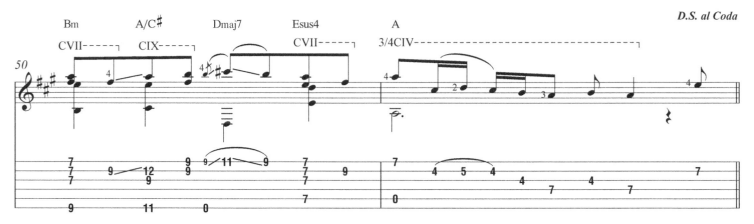

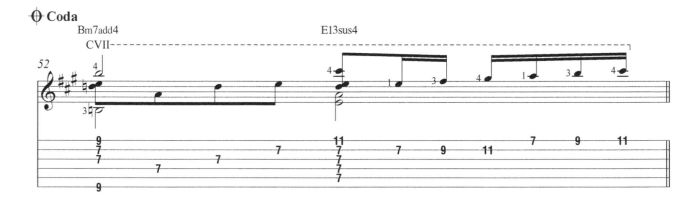

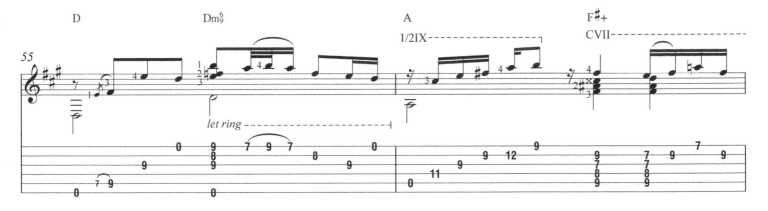

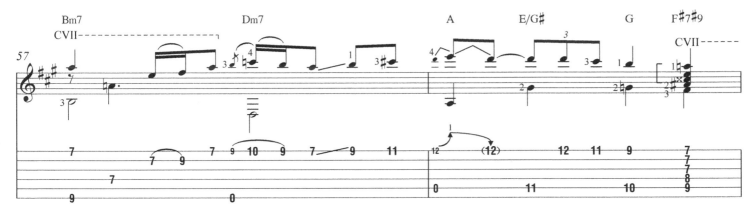

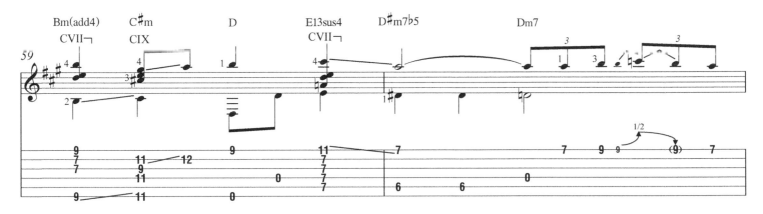

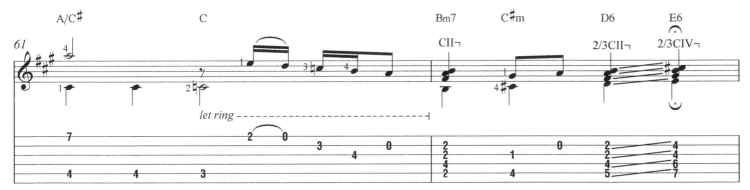

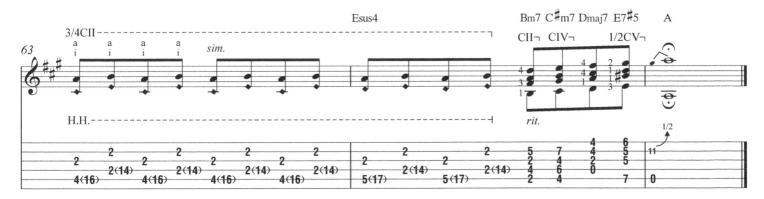

from *Under an Indigo Sky*

# Raining in My Heart

### Words and Music by Boudleaux Bryant and Felice Bryant

Tuning:
(low to high) D-A-D-G-A-D

Moderately ♩ = 112

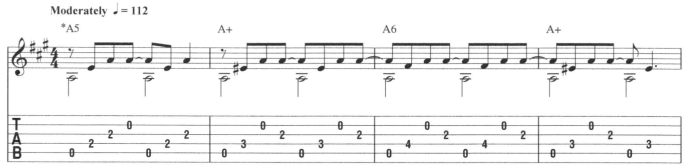

*Chord symbols reflect implied harmony.

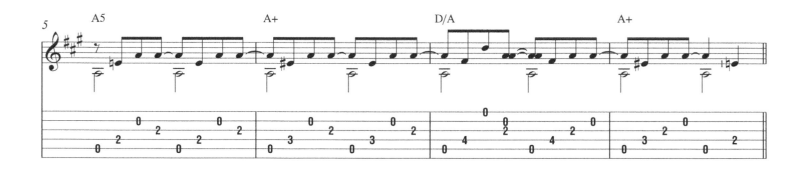

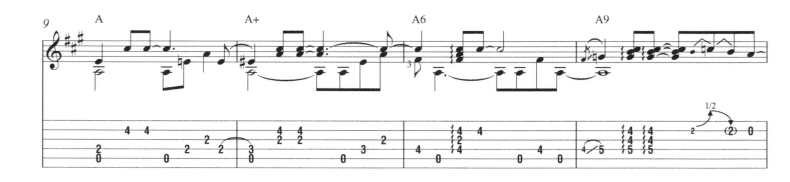

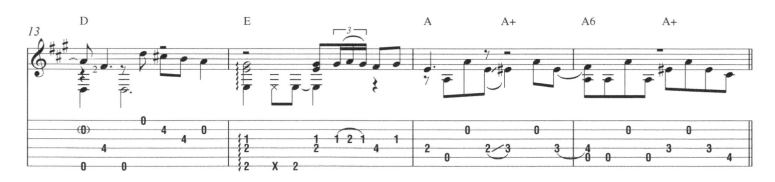

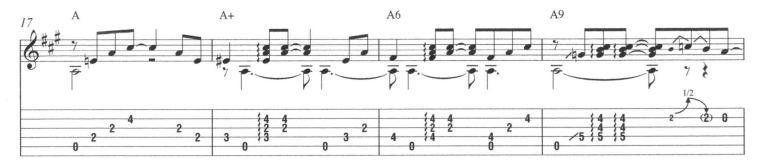

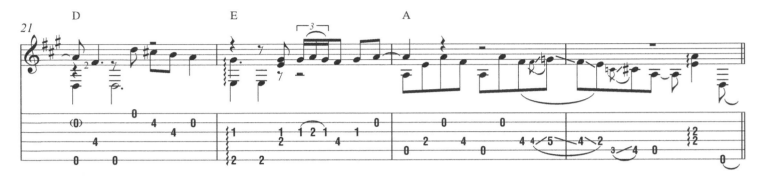

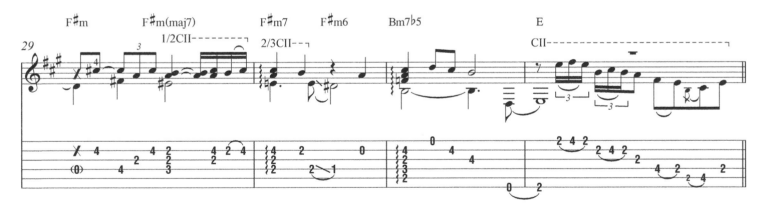

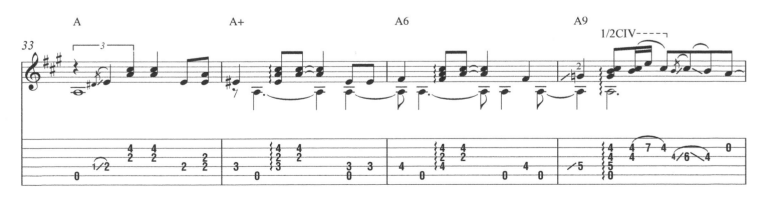

*Slap strings w/ r.h.

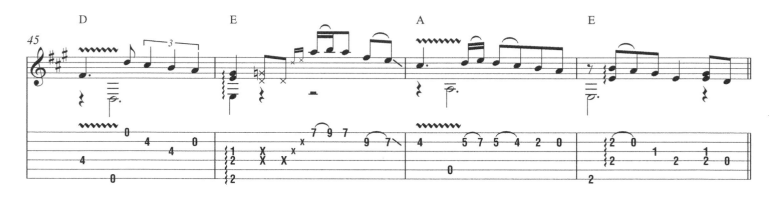

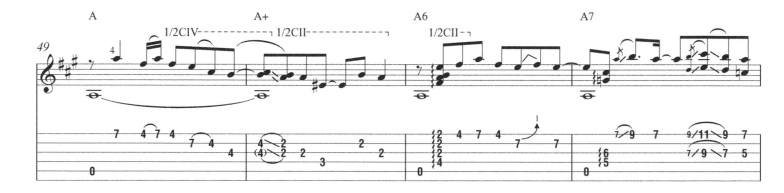

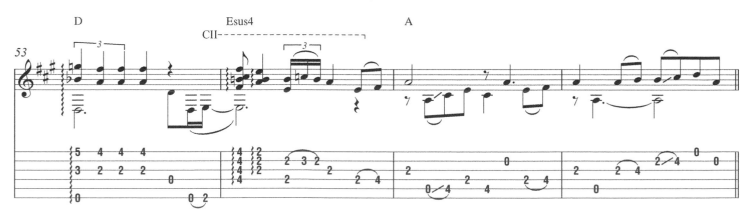

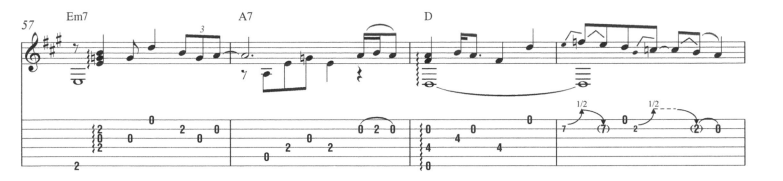

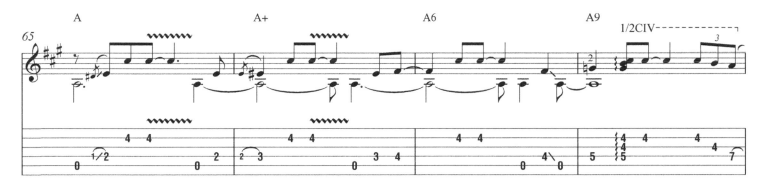

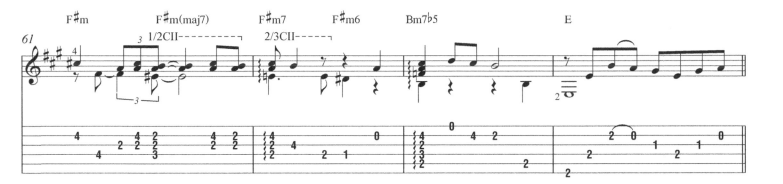

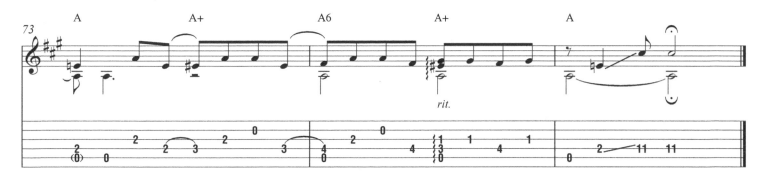

from *Under an Indigo Sky*

# Runaway

**Words and Music by Max Crook and Del Shannon**

Tuning:
(low to high) D-A-D-G-A-D

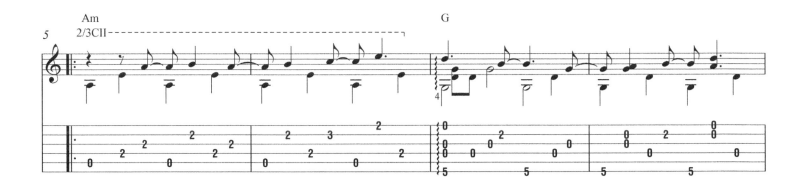

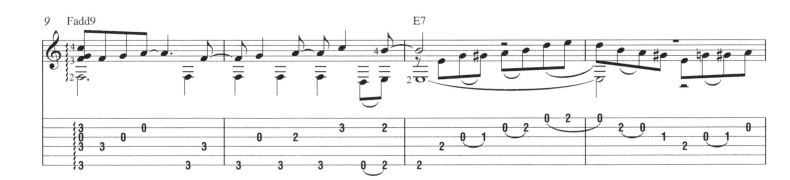

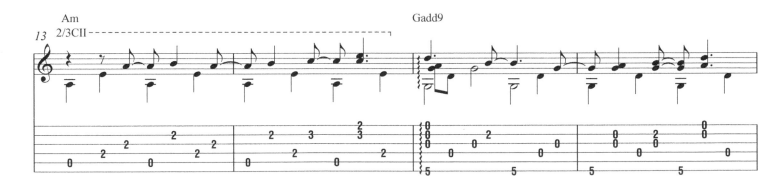

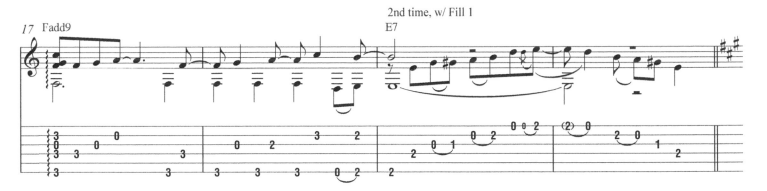

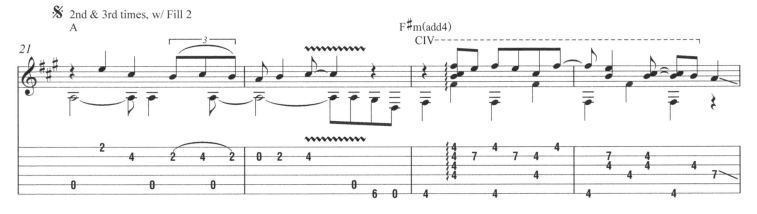

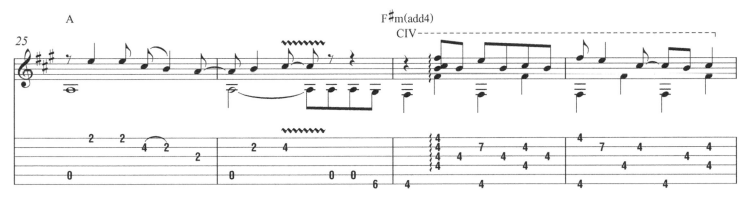

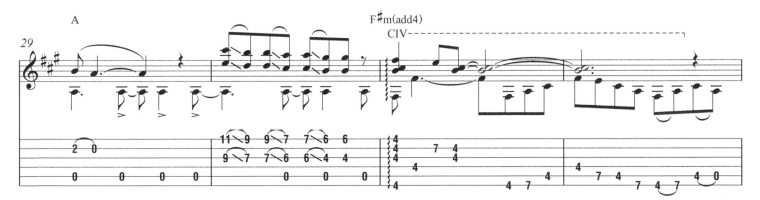

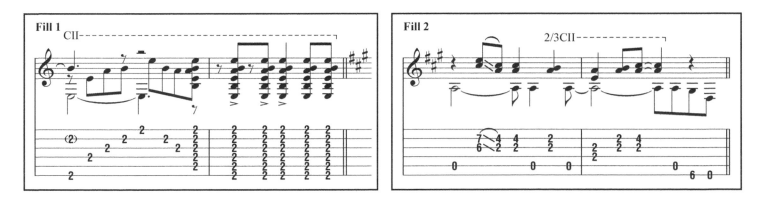

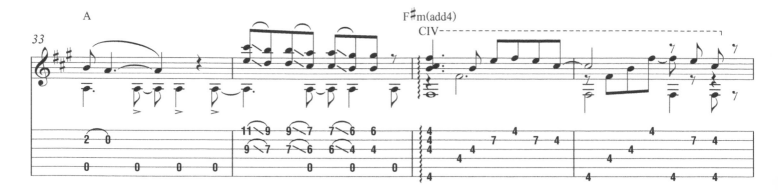

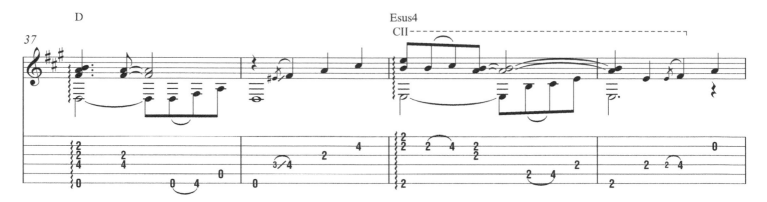

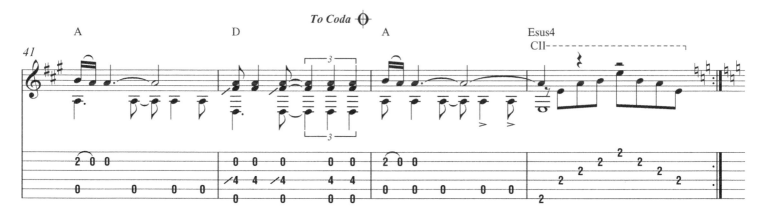

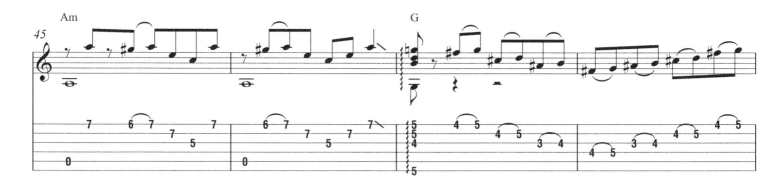

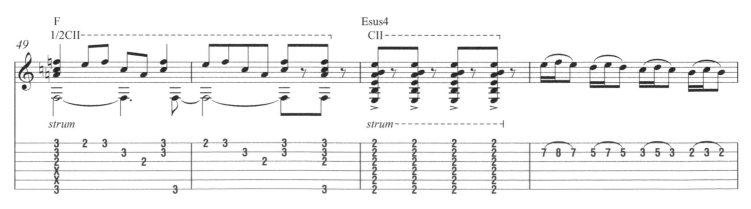

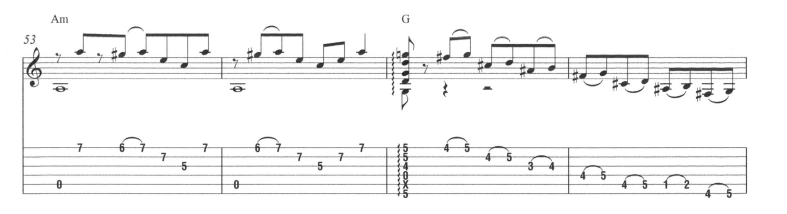

D.S. al Coda

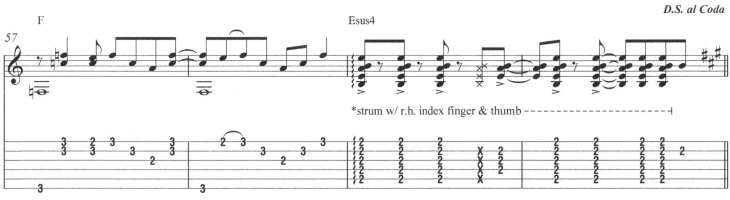

*strum w/ r.h. index finger & thumb - - - - - - - - - - - - - - - - - - - - - ┤

*"Pickless pick" – the index nail catches the downstroke
   and the thumbnail, the upstroke.

⊕ **Coda**

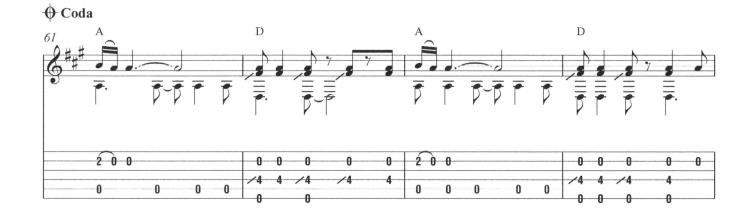

rit.

from *Fingerboard Road*

# (Sittin' On)
# The Dock of the Bay

**Words and Music by Steve Cropper and Otis Redding**

Tuning:
(low to high) D-A-D-G-A-D

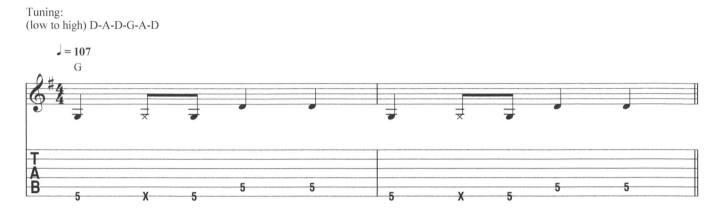

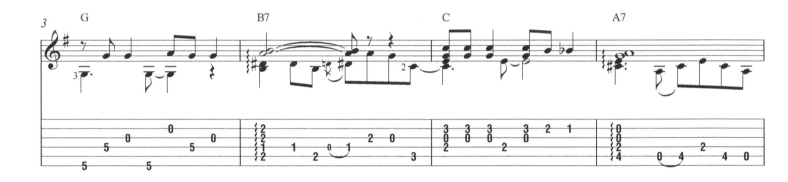

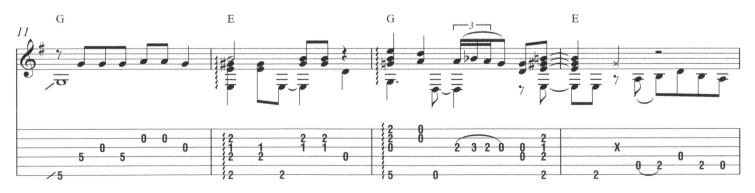

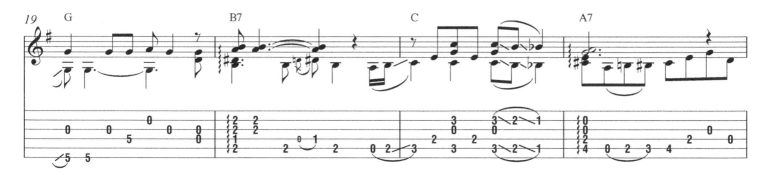

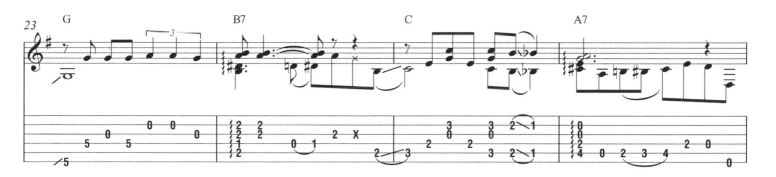

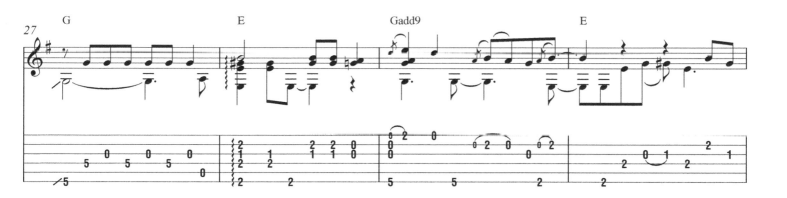

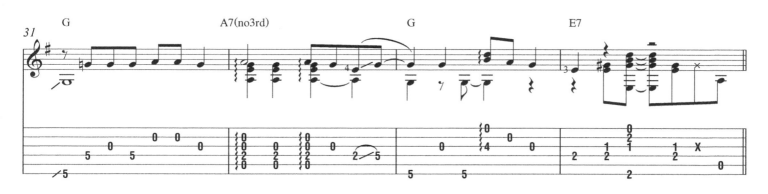

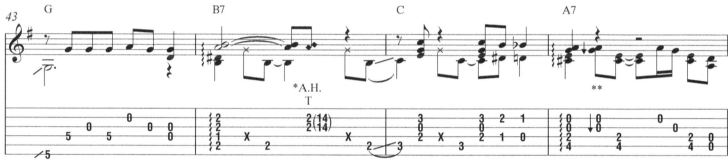

*Artificial Harmonic: The notes are fretted normally and harmonics are produced by the r.h. tapping the frets indicated in parentheses.

**Reverse rake w/ thumbnail

***As before

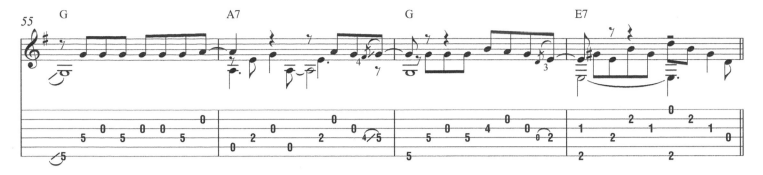

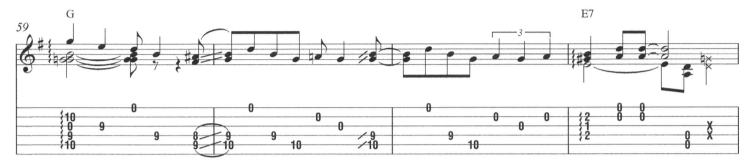

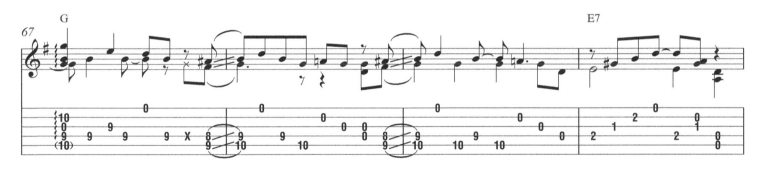

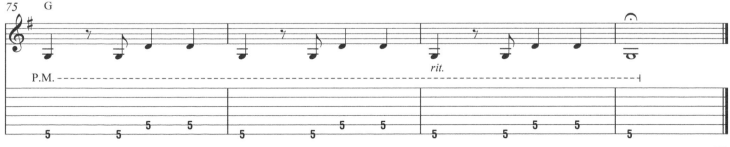

# Yesterday

### Words and Music by John Lennon and Paul McCartney

Tuning:
(low to high) D-A-D-G-A-D

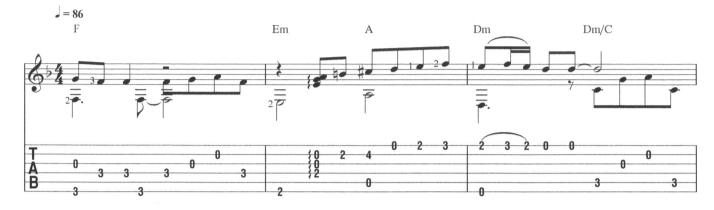

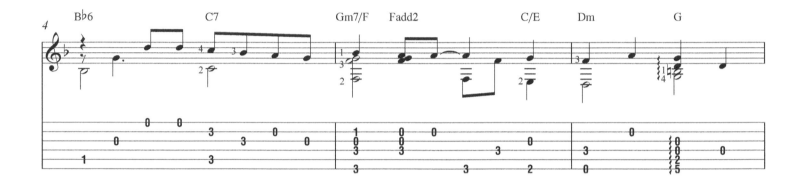

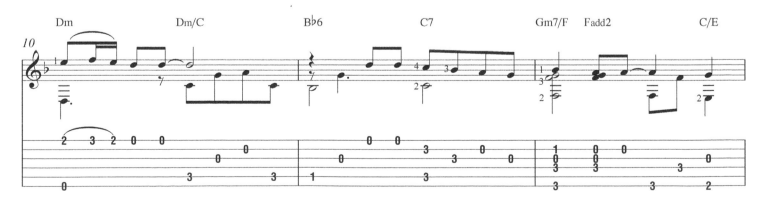

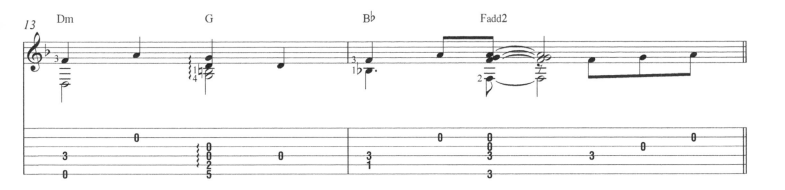

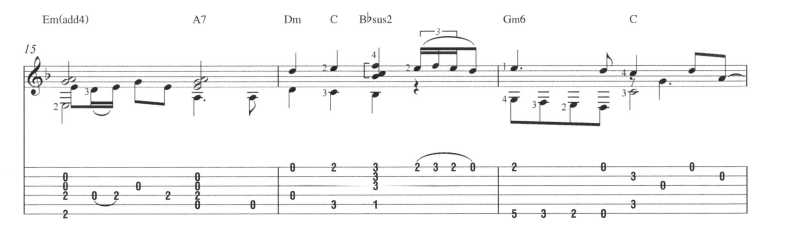

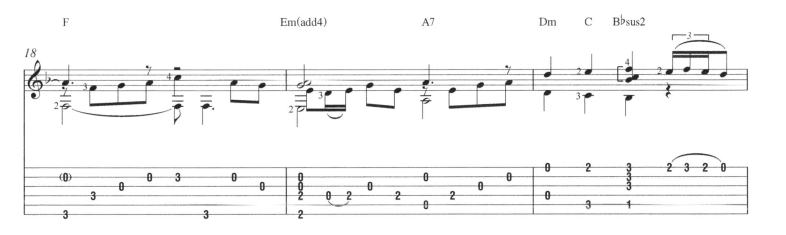

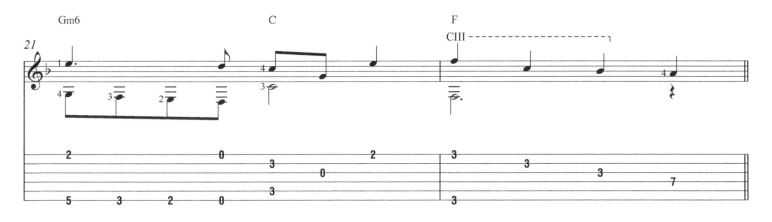

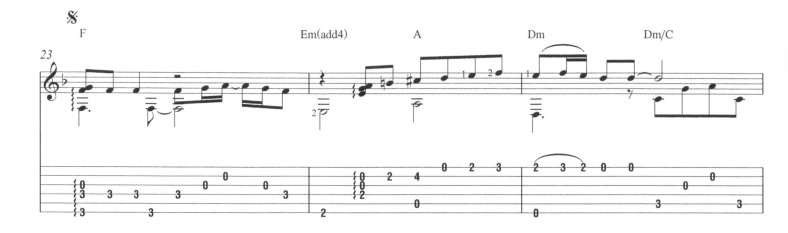

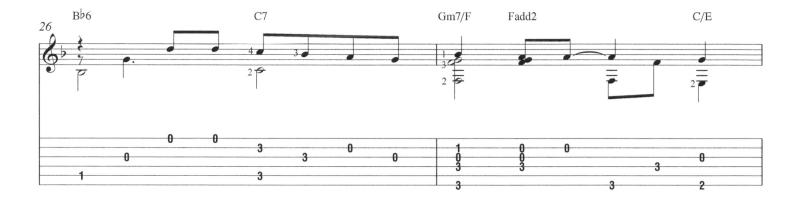

To Coda ⊕

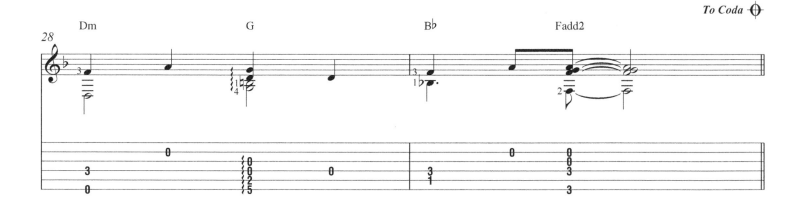

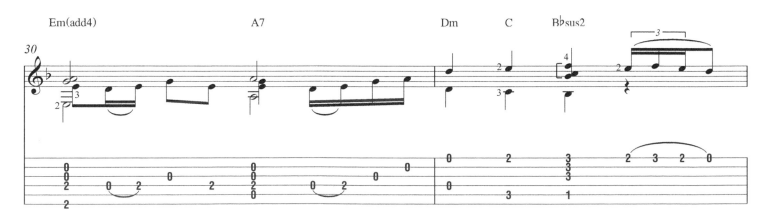

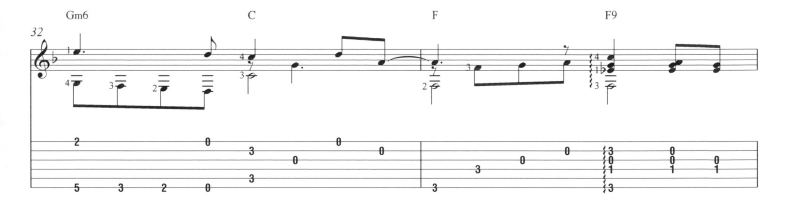

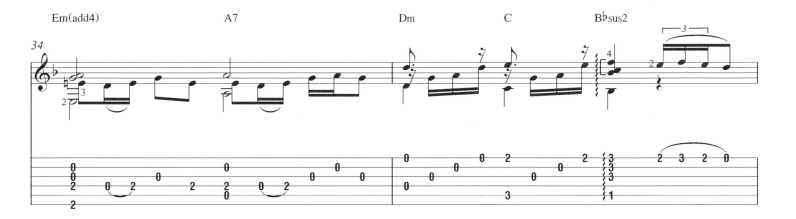

*D.S. al Coda*

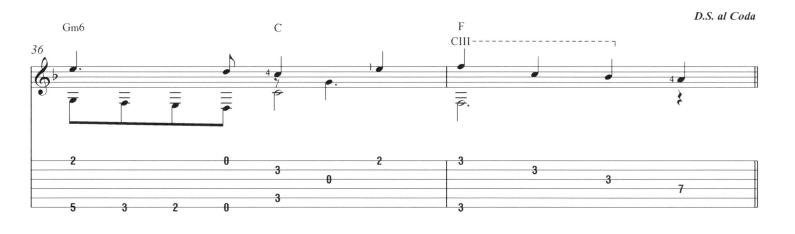

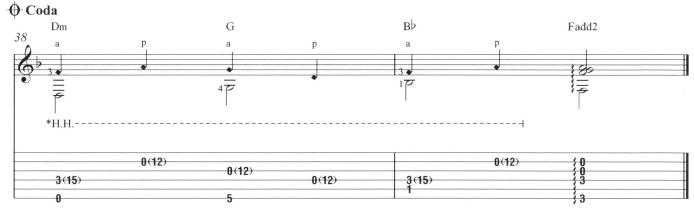

*Harp Harmonic: The note is fretted normally and a harmonic is produced by gently resting the right hand's index finger 12 frets (one octave) above the indicated fret while the right hand's thumb assists by plucking the appropriate string. This technique also applies to unfretted harmonics played at the 12th fret.

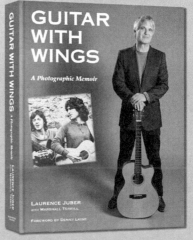